Essay Ind...

From an original sketch by F. J. Zimmerer

THE PORTMANTEAU THEATER

Prologue   Memory   Device Bearer

PORTMANTEAU PLAYS

BY

STUART WALKER

Edited, and with an Introduction by

EDWARD HALE BIERSTADT

ONE-ACT PLAYS IN REPRINT

ILLUSTRATED

Core Collection Books, inc.
GREAT NECK, NEW YORK

First Published 1917
Reprinted 1977

INTERNATIONAL STANDARD BOOK NUMBER
0-8486-2024-0

LIBRARY OF CONGRESS CATALOG NUMBER
77-70364

PRINTED IN THE UNITED STATES OF AMERICA

TABLE OF CONTENTS

ILLUSTRATIONS

INTRODUCTION

The Man

Especially during the last two decades in America various movements have been generated for the establishment of a more or less permanent repertory theater. In most cases these movements have proved abortive; indeed, they have always proved abortive whenever actual permanency was implied. The failure of the New Theater, now the Century Theater, in New York, marks the highest point in a long series of failures. Next in line for consideration comes Stuart Walker's Portmanteau Theater. So far it has been entirely successful, and at the present moment there is no reason for prophesying anything but unqualified triumph for the venture. But in any case, whatever time may do to controvert the present situation, the Portmanteau Theater has taught us not one, but many lessons, and it seems entirely fitting that an effort should now be made to sum up in detail the history of the theater, in order that a proper basis for future deduction may be furnished. To do this effectively it will be well to begin with the presiding genius of the Portmanteau, Stuart Walker himself.

Stuart Walker was born in Augusta, Kentucky, in the oldest house in that part of the State. The exact date of his birth is problematical, as Mr. Walker has so far persisted in maintaining a strict secrecy on the point. Whether he thinks that he is too old or too young, I do not know; very evidently he believes there is a " too " somewhere in that connection. It seems to me a safe conjecture, however, that he is about thirty-three years old. His father was a lumberman, and with this exception all Mr. Walker's forbears on both sides of the house were either lawyers or preachers. There is not a trace of the artistic, much less theatric, talent discernible in his geneology, and this is surely worthy of note considering his later career. The Walker family originates in North Carolina, not Kentucky, one of the chief reasons for the emigration being that one of Stuart Walker's ancestors had a family of twenty-two children. Naturally North Carolina felt the strain of so large a body of Walkers, and Stuart's forbear moved south near the blue grass country.

Mr. Walker's early childhood was uneventful. He was a strongly imaginative youngster. The chief point of interest during this period came as a more or less direct result of an attack of measles. It was at this time that his father gave him a toy theater in the endeavor to keep the boy indoors and quiet during his convalescence. He was just six years old. The theater was of German manufacture, and it had a green baize curtain, two sets of scenery, and real, though miniature, traps. There came with it also a play to be performed, but the play was written in German, and there was no one at hand who could translate German readily. So it was that Stuart's father made him an adaptation, a very free adaptation, of the " Bohemian Girl." This version was especially notable because it had two morals: the reward of virtue, and the condemnation of vice. Thus every one was satisfied. For six years the small boy gave regular performances of his one piece in the little theater, and then the audience rose in a body and demanded a change of bill. Here was a problem indeed for the Manager! Stuart rose to the occasion. He repainted the theater, changed the name of the play — and gave it over again. There was almost a riot. The question now was how to hold his audience, and the answer could be only one — repertory. The " star system " fortunately could not apply in this instance. And so Stuart wrote a play a week thereafter, and gave it on Monday afternoon just as he is doing today. The influence of this toy theater on Mr. Walker's future work can hardly be over emphasized. It taught him how to hold an audience, it suggested the importance of the repertory idea, and from a standpoint of stage mechanics it gave him material which he is using today. That will be taken up in detail a little further on. The plays he wrote for his fellows were designed to please — they had to please, and the experience gained through their manufacture and presentation has been an ever-present help up to now.

In 1890 the Walker family moved to Cincinnati. Here Stuart entered the elementary school, going from there to the High School, and to the University of Cincinnati, where he graduated in due course. While he was an undergraduate at the University he was one of the founders of the

Comedy Club, and this served to intensify his interests along the lines of the theater. It was at this time, too, that he came under the influence of Prof. George Miller of the English Department. It was through Professor Miller that Walker became first interested and then fascinated by the old English and Scottish ballads. Their dramatic power, their skill of narration, and their ability to make the auditor actually see and feel the events they recounted, made a deep and lasting impression. It was an early and primitive form of the dramatic art, this minstrelsy, and it suggested the fundamental principles of that art as perhaps little else could have done.

After his graduation from the University Mr. Walker was an invalid for several years. He had nothing to do but to think, and this formative period permitted the crystallization of ideas which had been germinating since boyhood. When he was strong enough, in an effort to recover his lost health, Mr. Walker went back south and worked some months in a great lumber camp. Here he came into contact with the Southern negro, and through him found again the ballad of his university days. At night, by the campfire, the darkies would chant their songs, each one taking up the theme in turn and acting out the story. Sometimes these assumed almost the proportion of impromptu plays — the Commedia dell' Arte over again! Mr. Walker listened, and learned. He has always been peculiar in his ability to reduce anything to its common denominator, and to put it into practical application. After his lumbering experience Mr.

Walker headed straight north to New York, and entered at the American Academy of Dramatic Arts. Now was the time for dreams to be realized.

After graduating from the Academy Mr. Walker played a summer in pantomime with Madame Alberti, and the following Autumn he applied for work at the Belasco offices. There he was taken on at once — at $12.50 a week — and William J. Dean, the general director for Mr. Belasco, told him he would have five lines to speak in a forthcoming production. The young Thespian banished thoughts of Hamlet — oh, yes, he had remembered that Booth was a Southerner — and took the part. The five lines were in " Is Matrimony a Failure? " and on the first night Walker was made assistant stage manager. After two weeks he was made stage manager of " The Lily " at $20 a week, and then on he went. He understudied all the important male parts in " The Lily " and in time played most of them, one night taking the place of Leo Ditrichstein who was ill. The next Autumn he went back to " Is Matrimony a Failure? " and played the part of the old man, but after two weeks he accepted the position of play-reader for Belasco. Next he was made stage manager of " The Concert," and manager of the Belasco Play Bureau. Again Mr. Walker took a step up, being made general stage manager; and all the time he was acting in whatever production of Mr. Belasco's he was needed. Shortly after this last move Mr. Dean became ill, and Mr. Walker took over his work contin-

INTRODUCTION

uing with it as general director for Belasco during the next year when he resigned to play for
a summer in stock with Jessie Bonstelle. The
following Autumn the Portmanteau Theater came
into being. This was in 1914 after Mr. Walker
had been with Belasco for six years. During
all this time there were people who, to use Mr.
Walker's own phrase, were "kind to me, and
told me things." Among these were first of all
William J. Dean whose friendly interest never
lessened, then W. J. Ferguson, James Bradbury,
Jane Cowl, and others in the cast of " Is Matrimony a Failure?"; in "The Lily," Nance
O'Neil, and Julia Dean, with Leo Ditrichstein,
William Morris, Bruce McRae, and Charles
Cartwright. But Mr. Dean was always the
greatest friend of all.

The average man after six years with Belasco
would have succumbed to the Belascian style of
production, but with Mr. Walker it taught him
largely what to avoid. He had his own stand-
ards on his entrance to the work, and he adhered
to them persistently, discarding whatever failed
to meet the test. Perhaps the most vital thing he
learned was how to train and handle actors, for
in this Belasco is a past-master. Also as director,
Mr. Walker came in close touch with a great part
of the "profession," and when his time came he
was able to draw upon his accumulated experience
to provide himself with a company. He saw how
the younger actors and actresses were passed over,
unless by some chance they were able to show their
talent, and he resolved that when his own day
dawned he would make his knowledge react to

their advantage and to his own. This made possible the incident that took place·just after the first performance of the Portmanteau when a very well-known New York manager rushed up to Mr. Walker and exclaimed, " Walker, where did you get that cast? I never heard of one of 'em before — but they're wonders! " Looking at him rather sadly Mr. Walker replied, " I got six of them out of your companies."

Chesterton remarks that the poet is the only really practical man, and this is certainly true of Stuart Walker. He has to a remarkable degree the power of materializing his own visions. His practical experience with the stage has not been wasted; he has dreamed, and he has made his dreams come true. Perhaps this is in part because of his great faith in them, but the concrete knowledge necessary to achieve their embodiment is there too. His taste, his judgment, are inherent, but the ability to make definite use of them has been arduously acquired.

THE THEATER

It was in the Autumn of 1914 that the idea for the Portmanteau Theater first came to Mr. Walker. He himself says that it came to him while he was taking a bath. This is so frivolous a statement that it is undoubtedly true. After all, stranger things have happened. Mr. Walker says, too, that the idea came to him as a complete vision, with every salient feature in its place just as it is now. This sounds like the poet talking, but even so that is no reason for doubting. At least *he* believes it. As a matter

of fact, like most visions, the idea came to birth
after a long period of almost unconcious incu-
bation, beginning no doubt with the toy theater
of childhood. Certain it is at any rate that when
Mr. Walker first came to New York he wanted
to do three things — to write, to act, and to produce plays, and it is equally certain that all these
three wishes were finally realized in the Portmanteau Theater.

Shortly after the idea had begun to take shape
in Mr. Walker's mind he went to a convention
of the Drama League where he met Mrs. Coon-
ley Ward with whom he discussed his new-born
project. Mrs. Ward took fire at once, so much
so in fact that she sent Mr. Walker on a tour
through the Middle West so that he might talk
publicly about the Portmanteau and gain some
idea of how such a theater would be received.
On this tour Mr. Walker met with instant response. He felt now that he was committed to
venture, and so without more delay he returned
to New York, built the theater and organized his
company. This was in the Spring of 1915.

According to Mr. Walker one of the first to
catch the spirit of the thing was William J.
Sheafe, Jr., and it was he who built the first model
for the theater. The first scene was made for
"Six Who Pass While the Lentils Boil," and
it was about this time that Frank J. Zimmerer and
Wilmot Heitland put in an appearance. Both
of these men did, and indeed are doing, splendid
work for the Portmanteau. It was Mr. Zimmerer who found the color for the theater itself,
and his stage settings for the plays of Lord Dun-

sany, as well as those for the plays of Mr. Walker, have since set New York by the ears. In every instance Mr. Walker has displayed an almost uncanny knack for getting just the right people to execute his ideas. This is indeed borne out in every phase of the work, artistic and mechanical. And again in almost every instance the people he has found have been hitherto quite unknown to the general public.

The proportions of the theater are based, according to the inventor's own statement, on the west wall of the apartment Mr. Walker occupied at that time, and this simply means that the proportions are, to a certain extent, arbitrary. Later they were worked out in greater detail as slight changes became necessary. The theater as it was finally built, however, was, and is, strictly according to Mr. Walker's primary conception.

The Portmanteau Theater is in direct descent from the toy theater about which so much has already been said. The structural outlines of the theater are largely the same, the same three color lighting system is employed, the stand-lights are used in exactly the same manner, and the improved reflectors are almost replicas. It was in the toy theater that Mr. Walker first learned that footlights cast unpleasant shadows, and he discarded them then. Later he relearned that lesson as well as others under Belasco, but they had first come to him years before. The greatest point of interest here, however, is that the lighting system for the Portmanteau Theater is unique. Mr. Walker can get effects with it that cannot be duplicated in any theater in the country.

INTRODUCTION

Yet this lighting system which has been hailed as so notable an achievement, as indeed it is, is based directly upon the system used in the little toy theater with the green baize curtain.

In 1915 Hiram Kelly Moderwell, author of "The Theater of Today" and at that time on the staff of the Boston *Evening Transcript* wrote an account of the Portmanteau Theater from which I shall quote at some length, for I cannot hope to better Mr. Moderwell's narrative.

"The Portmanteau Theater is a complete theatrical stage, somewhat smaller than usual, but ample for any play that does not make a special demand for 'bigness.' It can be set up in any room sixteen and a half feet high, twenty-five feet wide, and forty feet long (this length allowing for an audience of a hundred or more). Its walls support themselves by a resourceful system of interlocking, and ground bracing. They can be 'struck,' like scenery, by a few men, and boxed in an hour and a half. When boxed for shipping, the theater, with switchboard and all paraphernelia, weighs some 3,000 pounds, occupies 735 cubic feet, and can be loaded on to an ordinary hauling truck. The box of dimmers is a little marvel. It is forty-four inches long, thirty-two inches high, twenty-three inches deep, and weighs 350 pounds boxed. It can plug in on the ordinary 110 direct current system, which fact enables the theater to dispense with clumsy calcium devices. Mr. Walker dispenses altogether with footlights, not from necessity, but from choice. His lighting is obtained from movable spot lamps, and transparencies provide all needed coloring.

"The stage proper is sixteen feet high, eighteen feet deep, and twenty-two feet wide. The gridiron, from which scenery is hung, is a remarkable contrivance, light and flexible, but to all appearances quite free from all danger of breaking. A cloth cyclorama is hung on a semi-circular iron shaft, and is used for the background in out-of-door scenes, as in the best European theaters. There is an oblong fore-stage or apron in front of the proscenium and between two side entrance doorways, and here, in chummy nearness to his audience, Mr. Walker has large portions of his plays acted. The wings are ample for the storing of properties between scenes, and for the sojourn of actors awaiting their cues. Some of the framework of the stage is constructed of the actual boxes in which the rest is stored and shipped.

"Mr. Walker uses this stage with a keen sense of the beautiful. If he chose he could mount an ordinary realistic play in the realistic manner — the equipment will lend itself to that. But in the performances thus far given the producer has set himself to the exposition of his ideals of stagecraft. These are perhaps summarized in the formula: 'Imagination instead of information.' But Mr. Walker's personal taste narrows down still more toward the delicate and fanciful. And in this field at least, the Portmanteau should be able to equal any theater in America, provided only that the physical demands of the play be not exorbitant. The scenery in the Portmanteau is of the simplest description — back drops, ordinary sets, and a few properties. It is the lighting (which must in all imaginative work be a full half of the setting) that raises these prosaic things into the domain of magic. Mr. Walker's lighting is a simple affair of movable spots, nothing more. (We have Mr. Belasco to thank for showing us the marvels of the spot-light.) But by his extensive understanding of color in light, and especially of light against pigment, he produces effects of great beauty and distinction."

There are several points in Mr. Moderwell's account which may in the light of later events be clarified to advantage. It is interesting to remark that when the Portmanteau was set up in the Century Theater of New York Mr. Walker discarded the famous "million dollar switchboard" of the Century, finding that he could get better effects with his own switch-board, and little dimmer-box. The Century, that gigantic mausoleum of incompetency, is a monument to the conception that money can supply anything except brains. It should be noticed too that the forestage of the Portmanteau is unlike the conventional apron in that it is one step lower than the main or inner stage. When Mr. Moderwell speaks of the scenery as being " of the simplest description," he is speaking from a mechanical rather than from an artistic standpoint. Also it must be remembered that his account was written in the very early days of the Portmanteau before Zimmerer's gorgeous sets for the Dunsany plays, or for " The Birthday of the Infanta."

The fore-stage, and the inner stage of the

Portmanteau are lighted by four stand-lights —
two for each stage. These stands carry one lamp
each of 250 watts, behind which is an exceed-
ingly powerful mirror reflector. The two lights
for the fore-stage are placed down stage right
and left, and are masked from the audience by
screens. The two lights for the inner stage are
placed just inside the proscenium. It is evident
at once that there can be no question of unpleasant shadow effects with this method. As
Mr. Moderwell says, movable spots are used also,
but this is true only on occasion. Mr. Walker
relies on reflections, and color combinations to
bring most of his results. Heretofore to obtain
the diffuse light necessary for a full stage, bal-
cony spots have been used (Granville Barker relies on these to a great extent), but with the
single lamp used in combination with the reflectors
the Portmanteau manages to obtain a diffuse
light from nearby, a thing new in staging. I
have called these lights " stand-lights " because
they do not come under the head of any other
light used on the stage prior to their creation by
Mr. Walker. They differ from the bunch-light
simply in that only one bulb is used, and that the
reflector is an unusually powerful one constructed by Mr. Walker particularly for this purpose.

Mr. Walker's general theory of staging is very
simple. If you have a story to tell — tell it.
Do not bury it in a mass of detail which is unes-
sential. Go for the broad effects, the big outlines; the rest will be added as it becomes necessary. That is one of the things Belasco did *not*

teach the producer. You must remember also that the audience is an integral part of the whole. It must be willing to enter in and do its share. The part of an audience which will do this is worth working for, and the other part will come anyhow — they will follow the rest.

Simplicity is the keynote, and the knowledge when it will be more effective not to do a thing than to do it. "Nevertheless" is a masterpiece of omission, and it has been remarked that the characters of *Mother* and *Father* who never come on the stage at all are as real to the audience as the *Boy* or *Girl*. It is in connection with this play that some misguided people have tried to trace a tendency on Mr. Walker's part to return to the Elizabethan stage as the Device Bearer brings out the table, the lamp, and the chairs which go to make the set against the closed curtains of the inner stage. It is simply a question of practicability. The fore-stage cannot be curtained off, and as it must be set for this "Interlude before the Curtains" it is simply a matter of setting it in the most artistic way. Better the Device Bearer than the *Props* of the "Yellow Jacket" with his limp cigarette.

The point should be stressed again that Mr. Walker considers the audience and the stage as a unit. The fore-stage is significant of this attitude in the degree of intimacy it permits; indeed it may be considered as the connecting link between the stage proper and the auditorium. In some of Mr. Walker's plays the characters descend into the audience in the effort to weld the real and the make-believe into an indivisible

INTRODUCTION

whole. *Memory* as she walks down the center aisle to the stage, and the *Prologue* as he answers questions, both tend to carry out this theory. *You,* or the person in the audience, is of course a definite character in several of the plays, but sometimes a youngster in the house will pipe up and ask the *Prologue* questions on his own account. This never fails to fill Mr. Walker with joy, and the *Prologue* himself with perturbation, but so far the illusion has never been lost, no matter how severe a strain was put upon the ingenuity of the players.

Some persons, equally misguided with those before mentioned, have exclaimed that Mr. Walker in his attitude toward the audience has attempted to reinstitute some of the conventions of the Greek stage, and one critic has remarked that the "trick" was borrowed straight from vaudeville. The absurdity of both these statements is manifest. The consideration of the stage and the audience as a unit, and the effort to emphasize that point in every possible manner is as old as the stage itself. It is one of the early fundamentals of stagecraft, and the list would be endless of the times when it has been attempted. "The Knight of the Burning Pestle" is the most obvious example. There is not space here to elucidate this theory, but that it is of the highest importance is unquestionable.

In his directing, Mr. Walker makes certain demands, and adopts certain methods which are interesting, less in themselves, than in the results to which they give rise. He insists that every member of a cast shall know what the play is about.

He reads the play with them together and separately; he discusses it with them until all the individual conceptions become unified in the whole. One of his chief personal exactions is that actors shall be treated not as actors but as human beings, and the result is that every member of his company is a friend upon whom he can depend for the fullest support, and the heartiest coöperation. In rehearsing a new play Mr. Walker permits every one to work out his own ideas so far as it is possible (herein is a trace of the Belasco training), and a little later in the work the process of unifying the individual interpretations, and correcting them in so far as they need correction, is taken in hand. As a whole the Portmanteau company may be said to read excellently, that is, better than most American companies, and not so well as most English. Seldom a word is lost, and their reading of verse is quite remarkable considering what we are usually obliged to put up with. Both in diction and in enunciation the company will bear comparison with the best this country has to offer. Their acting is finished, and may be compared to the Irish Players in that the greatest effect is secured with the least effort. All this is to say that Mr. Walker has exhibited extraordinary ability in the training of his company. Every one of the young and unknown actors who have come into his charge has since received offers from Broadway managers, but only one or two have succumbed to the temptation.

Mr. Walker's effort is always to create through the audience rather than through the actors. He provides all the outline of illusion with all the necessary suggestion, leaving the audience to fill in the details for themselves. This places upon them a direct necessity for coming into the picture, to create for themselves, besides responding to the creation of others. And as I have said before, the part of an audience which will do this is worth working for — and it is no small part. In "Six Who Pass While the Lentils Boil" a great copper pot is placed on the fore-stage. The audience is told that the pot is on a fire and that it is full of boiling water. All through the performance the audience may be heard to gasp audibly whenever any one comes near enough to the pot to be in danger of being scalded. In "The Lady of the Weeping Willow Tree" a young girl kneels by the bank of a river crooning a quiet little song, as she sorrows over her mother. There is no river, and there is no action, and there is no mother, but, nine times out of ten, the audience have entered so fully into the spirit of the scene that they have been moved to tears. Can the realistic stage setting better this? It may be quite truly said that Mr. Walker has shown what can be done with the new stage art far more effectively than any other producer in America. In conception and in execution he has proved to the utmost that an ounce of artistic suggestion sympathetically applied is worth a pound of realistic reproduction. The first of these stimulates the imagination; the second stultifies it.

It must not be thought, however, that Mr. Walker is omnipotent or that the Portmanteau Theater is a cure-all for the woes of the stage.

INTRODUCTION

One becomes so surfeited with mediocrity that the advent of the new and beautiful is apt to be hailed as the very criterion of excellence, and consequently over-rated. Nothing could be more destructive to the well being of any movement than this attitude, for there inevitably follows in its wake a reaction which often undoes all the good that has been accomplished. The Portmanteau has very definite limitations. It cannot attempt to compete with the legitimate theater in many of its phases. Such competition is not necessary. The Portmanteau Theater has its place, and within the confines of its limitations it must exercise what influence it can bring to bear. It cannot be otherwise considered, and in my praise of its activities it must always be borne in mind that such statements are relative, not absolute. The Portmanteau stage is small, and is naturally not to be compared with a full-sized stage which is equipped with every device of contemporary stage-craft. It is in the acceptance of its self-imposed limitations, and in the turning of them to advantage that the Portmanteau derives no small part of its importance. It should be considered not in any sense as a Messiah, but simply as a Prophet.

The Plays

The first play in his present repertory which Mr. Walker wrote was "The Moon Lady," a pantomime written in 1908, six years before the theater itself came into being. The list of the other plays, all of them written especially for the Portmanteau, follows with the time of writing.

"Six Who Pass While the Lentils Boil,"
March 29th - April 1st, 1915.

"The Trimplet," June 26th - 29th, 1915.

"The Seven Gifts," a pantomime, December
7th, 1915.

"Nevertheless," December 31st, 1915.

"The Lady of the Weeping Willow Tree,"
February 6th - 16th, 1916.

"The Birthday of the Infanta," July 19th -
20th, 1916.

"The Very Naked Boy," September 3rd, 1916.

"The Medicine Show," September 5th, 1916.

It may fairly be said that although the ideas
for some of these plays had been in Mr. Walker's
mind for some time, they might never have
reached the dignity of paper had it not been for
the building of the Portmanteau. From the very
first Mr. Walker was strongly disinclined to use
plays without paying royalty, and his circum-
stances at that time did not permit such payment.
Obviously the only thing to do was to write his
own plays, and this he did.

The point of view from which the plays are
written is easy of explanation. Tell the story —
that is the sole secret; no, there is one other —
first have a story to tell. Mr. Walker denies
the charge of symbolism energetically, and herein
he is at one with Lord Dunsany who has suffered
under a like burden. For the most part we can
concur with Mr. Walker in his contention that
his plays are without ulterior motive: it is only
when such a frankly symbolic piece as "The
Trimplet" is brought into the discussion that we

waver. But "The Trimplet" stands alone after all in its symbolism, if symbolism it be. The story is the important part to Mr. Walker, and it is the important part to most of his audiences. If the others are able to get something more from the play so much the better, but the vital fact is that they get the story first. The symbolism is secondary when it is present at all.

At least half of the plays are social satires of a mild form, so mild indeed that one has almost to look for the satire. "Six Who Pass While the Lentils Boil" is the best example of this phase, as "The Trimplet" (unquestionably Mr. Walker's finest play) is the best example of his more purely poetic vein. "The Trimplet" deals with a certain magic thing which can cure all the ills of whoever finds it. The search and the finding constitute the action of the piece. "Six Who Pass While the Lentils Boil" is perhaps the most popular play in the Portmanteau repertory. The story is of a Queen who, having stepped on the ring-toe of the King's great-aunt, is condemned to die before the King's four clocks strike twelve. The Six who pass the pot, in which boil the lentils, are on their way to the beheading. "Nevertheless," an interlude played before the curtains on the fore-stage, tells of a burglar who reaches regeneration through two children and a dictionary. This play is a point of contention. It is liked and disliked in turn by critics and audiences. The key to the problem, however, is in the point of view which is brought to bear on the play. If one looks at it in the cold gray light of middle-aged inexperience it is doubtless a rather tedious trifle, but if one's eyes are those of childhood where " every one lives happy ever after " and an all-abiding faith in the ultimate fitness of things is the chief tenet of one's convictions — one will like the play. And this commentary is true in a greater or less degree of all Mr. Walker's work. " The Medicine Show " is a character study from the banks of the Ohio River. One does not see either the show or the river, but that does not matter. This play is a relic of the days in Augusta, Kentucky. Every word spoken by the three characters was heard at some time by the author as he lay, a small boy, on the banks of the great river. Its local color is exact to a degree, and its characterization is equally authentic, but that does not prevent it from being amusing. That it is true to life is well borne out by the fact that the play was received with the utmost enthusiasm in that part of the world where the characters were known and appreciated. New England took the piece coldly: *Giz* and *Lut'er* were too dirty for New England. " The Seven Gifts," a pantomime, was played for the first time in Madison Square, New York City, on Christmas night, 1915. The Theater was set up in the Square and a crowd of more than 5000 stood in the snow to see the performance. The players were warmed by heaters placed underneath the stage, and the heat so generated became at times so intense that they were in danger in being parboiled, though the temperature was near the freezing mark. Nevertheless the audience of 5000 stood patiently in the cold dark to which they were seemingly oblivious as they watched in fascinated wonder. "The Lady of the Weeping Willow Tree" is a play of old Japan, and many of the lines are taken from old Japanese songs, and legends with which the western world is not familiar. The play is a sad little tale; so sad, indeed, that I have known a hardened press-agent to weep over it as he read the manuscript. And a greater tribute than this would be impossible in my opinion! But though it is sad it is beautiful, and it is the only play Mr. Walker has written in more than one act. "The Very Naked Boy" is another interlude of rapid action. The play is not as fine as the others, however, either in conception or in the working out of the little episode on which it is based. "The Birthday of the Infanta," is an adaptation from a story of Oscar Wilde's. The original is full of dramatic incident and lends itself peculiarly to the treatment accorded it. The play has been successful from the very start. It is notable that Alfred Noyes used the same story for his poem "The Dwarf's Tragedy," one of his most poignantly beautiful creations. Mr. Walker's conception does the original full justice, and more than that no one can say. The staging of this piece is particularly fine with costumes by Mrs. John W. Alexander from original Velasquez portraits, and the set by Frank J. Zimmerer. Mr. Walker has several plays in preparation notably "A Leaf in the Wind," a peace play in which there is no mention of war, and "The Window Garden" the story of a little cripple in the slums of a great city. As will be seen by the list of plays with the dates of writing Mr. Walker is a rapid workman, but that is not always true. "The Window Garden" has been rewritten six times so far, but when it is done it will be as it was always intended.

Mr. Walker's attitude toward the writing of his plays, his emphasis on the importance of telling the story, may be traced in some part to the old English and Scottish ballads which influenced him so greatly in his earlier youth. The same fundamentals are apparent in each; the narrative, the color and clarity of outline, and the same tendency to bring the audience into active cooperation all proceed from the same source. But it is never plot for plot's sake with Mr. Walker. The plot grows out of the characters inevitably as it should grow, but the plot never controls the characters. It is characterization first, last, and all the time, and the characters tell the story. The length of the plays is entirely unconventional from a theatric standpoint. Some of them play twenty minutes, and some play fifty. It depends solely on the story that is to be told. There is neither cutting to make it shorter nor padding to make it longer. The play dictates its own length by its own requirements. It has been asked whether the plays have been influenced by the theater. Physically they have not. That is to say that the plays are in no sense unconventional because the theater itself is unconventional. Realistic plays could be staged in the Portmanteau just as effectively as the poetic and more fanciful drama. But it is quite probable that in writing his plays Mr. Walker has always thought of them in terms of the Portmanteau, though this does not mean that any very pronounced limitation has been imposed upon them. Rather otherwise, in so far as theatrical effects are concerned.

Mr. Walker, like Mr. Chesterton, does and says the extraordinary thing because it is the logical thing. Herein he is at one with the child mind, and herein lies no small measure of his importance. The creation of the *Prologue*, the *Device Bearer*, and the *You*, in the audience, bear witness to this very clearly. The *Prologue*, who answers questions from the audience, and *You* who asks them, have both a very definite reason. There are usually people in the theater who talk during a performance, thus making themselves a nuisance to all around them. One dislikes them because they distract one's attention from the stage, and too because one involuntarily tries unsuccessfully to hear what they are saying. Now we have questions asked and answered so that the whole theater can hear. The performance is undisturbed, and so is the audience. (There is discernible, however, a touch of satire in the conception.) And the Prologue to the Theater chanted by *Memory*, as well as the prologues to the separate plays spoken by the *Prologue* himself are for the people who must know exactly what it is all about. What better method could there be of telling them? The Prologue to the Theater is interesting in itself as having originally no connection with the Portmanteau. It was written in 1912 as the prologue to a book which was never published, and when the theater was built it became available. It is an exquisite bit of prose, comparable to Dunsany in its poetry of thought and of expression.

In his plays Mr. Walker has reached the same conclusion that every really worth-while, imaginative writer has reached in the course of centuries, namely that the child mind and the adult mind are fundamentally the same, and are thus subject to the same reaction and the same response. If the adult perception can once be induced to cast loose the bonds of custom, conventionality, and sophistry which have been grafted on imperceptibly through the course of years, and reach to the horizon of the child mind, we have every possibility of a very high form of art. A child reading a fairy tale perceives nothing beyond the story itself, and is consequently satisfied providing the tale be adequate, but the more mature intelligence immediately translates the characters and incidents into symbols of abstract qualities, acquiring thereby an emotional stimulus not only on the imaginative but also on the spiritual side. Sometimes this is carried to extremes and we have a frantic search for symbolism where none is intended, an inability to accept the story for the story's sake,— it is this among other things with which Mr. Walker is contending. The child mind is, relatively speaking, infinite, and the word infinite brings us at once to universality, that quality upon which all true art is founded as upon a rock. Mr. Walker has cut through to fundamentals in his work, and it is that which makes him worthy of especial attention. Only his terminology is strange, even while

INTRODUCTION

it possesses that delicate charm which only an artist with his point of view could give it.

I do not mean that Mr. Walker's type of play will be all things to all men. It will not, and cannot be, nor is it even intended that it should. It will always fall short on the purely intellectual side, and those persons who derive their sole enjoyment from an intellectual stimulus will always come away unsatisfied. Beyond question one of the reasons for the marked success of this type of play at present is simply that the inevitable reaction has set in against the play of pure observation as opposed to that of pure imagination. One side of our natures has been greatly neglected, and that side is now coming into its own as a plant blooms under watering. When the pendulum has swung too far we shall again react. It is unfortunate that only once in an age comes that genius who can combine successfully the seen and the unseen, the actual and the real. And although within their scope Mr. Walker's plays are of especial significance, that scope is admittedly small. One cannot compare " Alice in Wonderland " with the " Odyssey." And by the way, here is an interesting point — Mr. Walker has never read a line of Lewis Carroll; he has not even looked at the pictures! This absolves him of the accusation of imitation at any rate. It would be absurd to point out these pieces written for the Portmanteau as masterpieces either of literature or of the dramatic art, but within their scope, admitting their obvious restrictions, they are significant both in themselves and as an exposition of certain artistic theories of importance.

INTRODUCTION

THE RESULT

The first performances in the Portmanteau Theater were given at Christodora House, a settlement on Avenue B, New York City. The reason for this was that Mr. Walker had been interested in the activities of Christodora House for some time, and intended to establish there by means of the Portmanteau a community theater somewhat like the Neighborhood Playhouse in Grand Street. At the last moment, however, this idea proved impracticable, and several invitation performances were given instead to which professional people of importance were invited. The success was instantaneous. Critics, managers, and amateurs alike came, saw, and were conquered. The bill for these initial performances consisted of "The Trimplet," "The Six Who Pass While the Lentils Boil," and "A Fan and Two Candlesticks" by Mary MacMillan. The cast was composed of young professionals whom Mr. Walker had interested in the venture, and who in their enthusiasm contributed their services free of charge. It was worth their while to have such an opportunity of showing their talent, instead of remaining buried at the bottom of a Broadway company. Not one of them ever regretted the gamble if such it could be deemed. These performances were given on July 14th, 15th, and 21st, 1915, and from then on until Christmas Mr. Walker fought illness and prepared as best he could for the coming year. He now had the theater, the company, and sufficient plays with which to open a repertory season.

On Christmas night the Portmanteau was set up in Madison Square, and a performance of "The Seven Gifts," a pantomime, was given, and after this the Portmanteau took its place in the ranks. The first professional or paid performance was in Boston on February 14th, 1916, and after that the company was taken on tour through New England, as far west as Chicago, and as far south as Washington. The tour was somewhat in the nature of a triumphal march (in all my life I have never seen such notices and so many of them) and Mr. Walker brought his theater back to New York reinvigorated, and ready to try to crack the hardest nut of all — New York itself. By this time the Portmanteau had found its feet. In the Christodora House it had been tried on professionals, and had been eagerly accepted; now during the tour it had played in great cities, and in small towns, before audiences composed of the 400 and audiences composed of the 4,000,000, and it had gone equally well with rich and poor, young and old. Children adored the theater and the plays, and grown-ups had come to patronise and remained to applaud. It was now certain that a universal chord had been struck, and that success of the theater was assured.

In the summer of 1916 the Portmanteau was taken to Wyoming, New York, and here the new plays were tried out and the repertory for the coming season whipped into shape. The next October another and shorter tour through New England was arranged which was carried out with a repetition of the first success. It may be said here that fully nine-tenths of the initial bookings for the

INTRODUCTION

Portmanteau have been renewed, and in nearly every instance for a longer run than was first given. On November 27th, 1916, the Portmanteau opened at the Thirty-ninth Street Theater, New York, and after remaining there two weeks, changed to the Princess Theater just across the street, where it played until January 6th, 1917. It could have played out the season there except for the fact that bookings had been arranged which made it imperative to close at the stated time. After January 6th the theater started on a coast-to-coast tour from which it returns in April, and the history of which is yet to be written.

It had been considered highly undesirable to place the Portmanteau in direct competition with the Broadway theaters during the New York run, and so at the Thirty-ninth Street Theater there were no evening performances, and only four matinées a week, with one morning performance for children on Saturday. This last, however, was not successful and was shortly discontinued. On moving to the Princess Theater the demand was so great that Mr. Walker was obliged to play not only every afternoon, but also every evening, a total of twelve performances a week. And the houses to which the Portmanteau played were usually full. No mere fad could have made such a record. It is absolute proof of the intrinsic worth of the Portmanteau productions that the second largest and the most incredulous city in the world should have given it the response it did. The Portmanteau Theater was set on the stage of the larger theater, and this occasionally puzzled the audience, but there seemed no feasible method of obviating the difficulty though Mr. Walker labored long and earnestly at the problem. The New York run was rendered notable especially because of the production of three plays by Lord Dunsany two of which had not hitherto been performed professionally in America. The sets for these plays, as indeed the sets for the rest of the repertory, are surpassed by little that had been done in America so far. All but three of the sets have been made by Mr. Zimmerer who also did some of the sets for the Neighborhood Playhouse. Mr. Zimmerer has done all the sets and costumes for the Portmanteau productions with the following exceptions, the set for " Six Who Pass While the Lentils Boil " was made by William J. Sheafe, Jr., who also made the first model of the theater itself, and the costumes for the same play were designed by Wilmot Heitland who also designed the scenery and costumes for " Gammer Gurton's Nedle," and " The Lady of the Weeping Willow Tree." The costumes for " The Birthday of the Infanta " were designed by Mrs. John W. Alexander. With these exceptions Mr. Zimmerer has had the field to himself, and splendid use he has made of it. I do not intend in any sense to depreciate the work done by others in favor of Mr. Zimmerer — their achievements are too distinguished to permit that — but Mr. Zimmerer as a member of the company, and as scenic director of the theater is surely entitled to the major portion of the credit.

It was early in 1916 when Mr. Walker placed

INTRODUCTION

the business management of the Portmanteau in
the hands of Maximilian Elser, Jr., and Russell
Janney, both of them young, enthusiastic and
entirely fitted to assume such control. And just
here let me say that any rumors concerning the
financial backing of the Portmanteau by any one
are entirely without foundation. That is one of
the most remarkable and important features of
its progress. At the outset Mr. Walker borrowed $3,000 on his personal note, and at a ruin-
ous rate of interest, and up to December, 1916,
every penny that was put into the Portmanteau
came out of Mr. Walker's own pocket. He
received offers of backing time and again, but he
refused them because he felt that his salvation
lay in perfect freedom. With the exception of
the $3,000 mentioned the Portmanteau paid its
own way. It did more than that. In the Spring
of 1916 it showed a profit of twenty per cent. on
the investment to date. And yet it is an " uncommercial " theater! Surely it is uncommercial
in that it does not cater to " the tired business
man," but just as surely the theater is commercial
from a financial standpoint. It has not been able
to pay for the mass of publicity accorded other
productions, but no other production has been
given the enormous amount of publicity accorded
the Portmanteau. And that is because it is important in itself, able to stand on its own feet, and
make its own way in the world.

The response to most of the plays has been very
even no matter what the character or the situation
of the audience, but one or two of the plays
present rather amusing problems. " The Trimp-

let " is one of the favorite pieces with the public. It has always gone well, yet it is the one piece the critics unite in damning! And too " Gammer Gurton's Nedle," the earliest example of English comedy, included in every university course on the history of the drama, has been a failure from the start in the colleges, but has taken by storm New York, where it was played nineteen times in two weeks. Strange, is it not?

Particularly in view of what I have already said about the stage settings for the Portmanteau productions, it is interesting to note what some of them cost. One play cost nothing whatever to stage, one play cost $52, one cost $300, and one cost $1500. It is not necessary to go all through the list, for these four are representative. It should be observed, however, that the play with practically no setting at all, which cost nothing, has had a success equal to that of the play that cost $1500 to produce (which sum is the largest ever expended by Mr. Walker on a production).

I desire again to make here the point that the appeal of the Portmanteau has not been confined to any one class or to any one age of persons. It is this peculiar universality of appeal which makes the Portmanteau of importance both from a theatric and dramatic standpoint. I should like also to point out one thing that I have noticed about Portmanteau audiences,— men are quicker to get into the spirit of the thing than women. The women are usually a little hesitant, and self-conscious, while the men lose all thought of self in their enjoyment of what is before them. Perhaps this is because men always retain a large,

healthy strain of the " little-boy " spirit while
women have but little if any of the " little-girl."
And too a little boy is a known and loved factor
in the scheme of things, but a little girl — is there
such a thing?

The reason for the Portmanteau Theater itself
as differentiated from its productions may be easily summed up in the statement that it permits its
director absolute freedom.   He can in an almost
literal sense take up his theater and walk.   He is
bound down by none of the inconveniences that
beset the ordinary play house.   When he goes on
tour his scenery always fits the stage because it is
always the same stage.   He can play where there
is no theater if there is a hall, or a barn or a ball-
room in which he can set up his equipment.   I
have been asked whether in the original conception
of the Portmanteau there was not an auditorium
included.   No, never.   And hence in a certain
sense the Portmanteau is not a theater at all.   It
is simply a stage with all the appurtenances of one.
The Portmanteau Theater proves once for all
how easily and simply, and yet how artistically
and effectively, things can be done.   It is not
" highbrow " any more than it is the opposite.
It is for everybody.   The Portmanteau has
shown us that a very high form of art can be pro-
duced at a very low cost.   And it has shown that
whatever the cost the thing that is really worth
while will more than pay for itself.

The future of the Portmanteau is another question.   It may be that in the due course of time
Mr. Walker will permit other theaters to be built
from his plans, and we shall have the travelling

theater as a fixture in our theatrical life. When this becomes possible it will engender a spread and growth of the new stage art which would otherwise have been impossible. One of the most vital things the Portmanteau Theater has given us so far, is probably the best repertory company in America. And this is after all what Mr. Walker is working for most. Books have been written without end on the necessity of the repertory theater. The experiment has been tried and tried again, and in most instances it has failed. But from the Theatre Libre to the Abbey Theater all these experiments have left their mark, have emphasized again the necessity for such a move, and have brought us one step nearer to the goal. And too, the traveling repertory theater has twice the chance of success that a stationary theater has. It is not necessary that the repertory imply the " little " theater, though that has its undeniable place. The ideal seating capacity of a theater is from 500 to 750, and the size of the ideal stage is that of the Princess Theater, New York. The proportions of the Punch and Judy Theater, New York, are excellent in every way, but this is exclusive of the stage itself. The auditorium should be deeper than it is wide, and no wider than the stage. The whole stage picture should always be in full view of every one, and every one should see it from approximately the same angle.

Before leaving the Portmanteau Theater let me call attention to another point of importance. The full quota of sets for the theater along with the theater itself can be transported at the cost, or less than the cost, of transporting the scenery alone of an ordinary production. And, in addition, there is no house rent to pay, the biggest item of all, when the theater reaches its destination. True it must have its hall or auditorium of some kind, but that is not a drop in the bucket compared with what most managers have to pay for the use of a completely equipped theater. And the Portmanteau has its own lighting system and everything else it needs. If only because of this one factor of expense, the theater has more than justified its existence. With such an equipment the young man whose principal assets are taste and judgment can afford to embark on a managerial career unhampered by the thought that he will have to invest a fortune before he sees the first profits. If the Portmanteau eventually tends to take the theater out of the hands of those entirely unfitted to control it, and helps to restore the balance of power by bringing the younger and more idealistic element into the field, it will have performed an epoch-making task.

By all this it will be seen that the Portmanteau Theater and its plays cannot be considered quite together. The theater itself means much artistically and commercially. It is in itself an emancipation proclamation, for it means freedom of movement, and vastly increased opportunities. It is the modern version of the strolling players. It has given us a lighting system unequaled in its simplicity and unrivaled in the ordinary theater. The settings for its plays have been masterpieces of stage art. The theater itself and the effects which it has engendered are thus of the utmost importance in the development and history of the stage.

The plays contained in the repertory of the theater, of which there is a list in the Appendix, are of like importance in the scheme of things, perhaps not in themselves but in the trend which they indicate. We are unquestionably upon the eve of a great romantic renaissance. Woe to art if this be not so! The stage craft of Craig, of Reinhardt, and of Barker has marked the romantic renaissance of the theater; surely the drama cannot do otherwise than follow. Naturalism is to be considered as a necessary purgative rather than as a healthy, normal condition of the artistic structure. "The Gods of the Mountain" of Lord Dunsany, and "The Trimplet" of Stuart Walker are quite as "real" as "The Fugitive" of Galsworthy. Their terminology is different, that is all. That which is true of man in the mythical city of Kongros is likewise true of him in London. I do not mean to argue in favor of the abandonment of the play written in terms of every-day life, such as Galsworthy's, in favor of the purely imaginative, and poetic drama. Such an abandonment would be as futile as it would unwise. But I do mean to point out that the abnormal intellectualization of art is fully as destructive to the vital spiritual quality as the etherialization of art would be to the necessary intellectual quality. The Scriptures bid us to be as little children. We *are* as little children, and the virtue lies not in the fact itself, but in our realization and acknowledgment of it. It is only when we endeavor to assume the raiment of deities that we are overtaken by the seven green gods of Marma and punished for our temerity — or that Mr. Shaw, who also is a prophet in his own way, is able to point the finger of scorn at us, wise in our folly.

In all that I have written here it will be very evident that I have dwelt on the excellencies of the Portmanteau Theater and its plays rather than on the weaknesses. Surely that is but natural. It must not be thought, however, that there are no weaknesses, that there is no room for improvement, or that the last word has been said on the subject. (Indeed it is one of the most vital factors, that only the first word has been said.) I have endeavored to sum up here what the Portmanteau has done as well as what it is, but by far the most important question is what it may do, and what it may become. It may be that the influence it will finally exert will be largely indirect, that the others who come after Mr. Walker will lay the surface on the road bed he has worked over. Only Time will show that, and Time is jealous of his secrets. But at least we have been shown something new, something worth while, and so it is well to pause and consider not only what it does mean, but also what it may mean in the final working out of the scheme of things. What will the travelling theater, the portable stage, mean to the repertory movement? Something beyond question. What does the drama of imagination as opposed to that of observation indicate, and where will it lead us? Surely it is worthy of consideration. Hence it must again be borne in mind that the importance of the Portmanteau, and it is important, is entirely relative, not absolute, that while it is deeply suggestive it is not in any sense conclusive, and that it is far less what the Portmanteau is now than what we shall make of it in the future that must concern us.

And so when Memory draws slowly back the deep blue curtains of the Portmanteau Theater, and bids us come with her through the portals of " once upon a time, but not so very long ago," it is good to grasp our faith very firmly and to go with her, for there we may find not the surface things of every day life, but the deeper things. We may even find Truth. And we may even find that Truth is beautiful.

EDWARD HALE BIERSTADT.

THE PROLOGUE TO THE
PORTMANTEAU THEATER

As the lights in the theater are lowered the voice of MEMORY *is heard as she passes through the audience to the stage.*

MEMORY

Once upon a time, but not so very long ago, you very grown-ups believed in all true things. You believed until you met the Fourteen Doubters who were so positive in their unbelief that you weakly cast aside the things that made you happy for the hapless things that they were calling life. You were afraid or ashamed to persist in your old thoughts, and strong in your folly you discouraged your little boy, and other people's little boys from the pastimes they had loved. Yet all through the early days you had been surely building magnificent cities, and all about you laying out magnificent gardens, and, with an April pool you had made infinite seas where pirates fought or mermaids played in coral caves. Then came the Doubters laughing and jeering at you, and you let your cities, and gardens, and seas go floating in the air — unseen, unsung — wonderful cities, and gardens, and seas, peopled with the realest of people. . . . So now you, and he, and I are met at the portals. Pass through them with me. I have something there that you think is lost. The key is the tiny regret for the real things, the little regret that sometimes seems to weight

3

your spirit at twilight, and compress all life into a moment's longing. Come, pass through. You cannot lose your way. Here are your cities, your gardens, and your April pools. Come through the portals of once upon a time, but not so very long ago — today — now!

She passes through the soft blue curtains, but unless you are willing to follow her, turn back now. There are only play-things here.

THE TRIMPLET

The Lady Bobolara
The Marquess of Strenathco
The Lady Caratina
The Baron Milton-Maurice
The Person Passing By
You (in the audience)

The Scene is a lonely place.
The Time is partly then and partly nowadays.

[When Memory has disappeared and the blue curtains are quite still and every one who is old and irrevocably very grown-up has left the theatre, the Prologue of the Plays and the Device-Bearer appear at either side of the forestage. Then the Prologue speaks.

PROLOGUE

She was Memory ... I am the Prologue ... He is the Device-Bearer ... I am here to elucidate —

YOU

What is elucidate?

PROLOGUE

Elucidate means to make clear, to explain anything you do not understand. . . . As I said, I am here to elucidate everything you are not sure about. I shall answer questions sometimes, but not always. . . . Our first play is a dream play and you know what you ought to think of a dream. At first it all seems very strange, and so many things happen that you think you can not possibly remember all the events. Then suddenly something snaps — and everything becomes as clear as the day which is coming over the sea with your bath and your breakfast. Now, you won't spoil a dream by asking questions, will you?

[He claps his hands twice for silence and with a very polite bow he and the Device-Bearer withdraw.

7

*When the curtains open the stage is empty.
The lights which seemed indistinct and blurred
at first, gradually increase until trees form
against a luminous and misty, moonlit sky.
Presently a voice is heard calling far away —
the voice of The Person Passing By.*

VOICE
Halloo!   Hoola!
[*Enter the Lady Caratina.*
*She is young and eager with a note of tragic fear
in her voice.*

CARATINA
To-day I am one and twenty.   To-day I come to
this lonely place to learn my future.   I must
know how to live happily ever after.   My
mother says if I call aloud a voice will answer
and tell me how I may live happily ever after.
Halloo!   Hoola!

VOICE
Halloo!   Hoola!

CARATINA
A voice!   A voice!   The voice of The Person
Passing By.

VOICE
Halloo!   Hoola!

CARATINA
The voice of The Person Passing By! . . .
Speak to me.

VOICE
Halloo!   Hoola!

CARATINA
My mother, the Lady Bobolara, bade me come
to you.

8

THE TRIMPLET

VOICE
  Halloo! Hoola! (*The voice seems to come from one afloat in the air*)
CARATINA
  Can you hear me?
VOICE
  Halloo! Hoola!
CARATINA
  Then these magic words I say:
  Mullion! Mizzen!
  The moon has risen
  And only one star is near;
  The mist has spread
  From its valley bed,
  Oh, Passer, do you hear?
VOICE
  Plucky! Plenty!
  You're one and twenty —
  Is there something you would know?
  This is your choice,
  To hear my voice,
  Speak truth or naught, or go.
CARATINA
  Belith! Belath!
  I've followed the path
  That leads to this lonely place.
  For hours — full nine —
  I've climbed to the shrine
  Where I hope to see your face.
VOICE
  You can not see
  The face of me
  Until the wild bird sings.
  Five tests I make

9

For pity's sake.
For dreams and finger rings.

CARATINA

Mullion! Mizzen!
The moon has risen
And only one star is near —
The mist has spread
From its valley bed,
Oh, Passer, I am here.

VOICE

Can you feel?

CARATINA

I can feel.

VOICE

What do you feel?

CARATINA

I feel the chill of the air and the damp of the mist, and the magic of the moon — and a great, great love for Milton-Maurice.

VOICE

You can feel. . . . Can you taste?

CARATINA

I can taste.

VOICE

What can you taste?

CARATINA

I passed a lovely tree upon the way, and I tasted of the fruit that was delicate like the honey from a forget-me-not.

VOICE

You can taste. . . . Can you hear?

CARATINA

I can hear the tall trees whisper to the little winds.

VOICE

You can hear. . . . Can you see?

CARATINA

I can see yon tall, tall tree touch on the nearest star.

VOICE

You can see. . . . Can you smell?

CARATINA

I can smell the hideous mould of the dead leaves that hide amongst the trees.

VOICE

You can not smell.

CARATINA

I can smell the death-like smell of mould.

VOICE

There is a surpassing fragrance of a thousand trees that fills the air.

CARATINA

I can not smell. . . . Alas, I need your help.

VOICE

I can not help until you see my face.

CARATINA

I can not see your face until the wild bird sings.

VOICE

I have nothing more to say.   Halloo!   Hoola!
(*The voice is lost in the distance*)

CARATINA

Alas, my mother comes and I have naught to tell.   My future lies in mystery.   I am one and twenty, and still I do not know how to live happily ever after.   (*She sits and weeps*)
[*Enter the Lady Bobolara.*
She is an alert, hard woman with an undertone

*of resignation. She has come to the lonely
place because she has always come, but she feels
that her pilgrimage is futile.*

BOBOLARA

Halloo!   Hoola!

VOICE

Halloo!   Hoola!

BOBOLARA

Mullion!   Mizzen!
The moon has risen
And never a star is near;
The mist has spread,
From its valley bed,
Oh, Passer, do you hear?

VOICE

Plucky!   Plenty!
You're three times twenty,
The days will come from afar
Until you see
Yon tall, tall tree
Touch on the nearest star.

BOBOLARA

I can not see
Yon tall, tall tree
Touch on the nearest star.

VOICE

One test I'll make
For pity's sake
For dreams and a silver bar.

BOBOLARA

Mullion!   Mizzen!
The moon has risen
And never a star is near;
The mist has spread

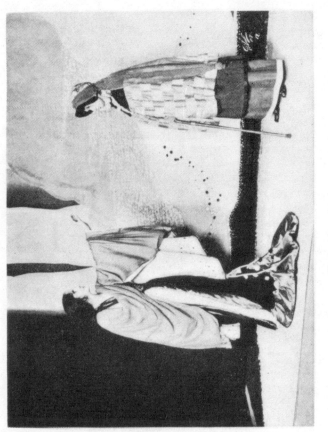

"THE TRIMPLET"

Caratina and her mother, Bobolara

From its valley bed —
Oh, Passer, I am here.

VOICE

Can you see?

BOBOLARA

I can feel, and taste, and smell, and hear, but I can not see yon tall, tall tree touch on the nearest star.

CARATINA

Mother, I can see yon tall, tall tree touch on the nearest star.

BOBOLARA

It does not touch. I see trees and hills and sky — trees like jagged teeth bite into the sky. (*She has seen this so often she does not look*)

VOICE

See, your daughter weeps.

BOBOLARA

Her eyes are in the shadow. I can not see them.

VOICE

So parts of the whole, wide world are always in shadow.

CARATINA

Mother, I am going to search for the wild bird and beg him to sing.

BOBOLARA

Since I was one and twenty I have waited for the tall, tall tree to touch on the nearest star.

CARATINA

The tall tree is touching on the star now, Mother dear.

BOBOLARA

Silly girl! The tree and star are miles apart.

CARATINA

Come here and you will see.

BOBOLARA

Why should I go there? They do not touch, I say.

CARATINA

But I see them touch.

BOBOLARA

Impudent girl!

CARATINA

I know what I see.

BOBOLARA

The still, tall trees do nothing but waft their fragrance in the air.

CARATINA

I do not smell a fragrance. The air is filled with the smell of mould that the sun has never warmed.

BOBOLARA

I say there is a fragrance from the trees.

CARATINA

I shall not say there is no fragrance, Mother dear, but until I come face to face with The Person Passing By I can not learn to smell the fragrance. I shall find the wild bird, and beg him to sing.

BOBOLARA

The wild bird will never sing.

CARATINA

I shall find the wild bird, Mother, and when he sees my tears he will sing. (*Caratina goes out*)

BOBOLARA

He will never sing.

VOICE
  You do not know, old woman. Let her go.
BOBOLARA (*fiercely; facing the unseen*)
  Why have you kept me waiting all these years?
VOICE
  I have not kept you waiting. You have kept
  yourself waiting. You will not see, and you
  have grown bitter.
BOBOLARA
  Is there naught else for me to do but wait?
VOICE
  To-day your daughter is one and twenty. To-
  day Milton-Maurice is one and twenty. He
  comes to me to learn his fate. What shall I
  say?
BOBOLARA
  He can not wed my daughter.
VOICE
  Why?
BOBOLARA
  His father and I have not spoken for nine and
  thirty years.
VOICE
  Why?
BOBOLARA
  His father injured my father.
VOICE
  Did he injure you?
BOBOLARA
  No, but I hate him because he is his father's son.
VOICE
  Hatred will not heal the hurt.
BOBOLARA
  Oh, if I could see you face to face!

VOICE
    Your eyes are blind,
    Your heart is blind,
    Your life has been a life of ruth;
    Your eyes can't see
    The truths that be
    Until your heart sees truth.

BOBOLARA
    Oh, if I could only see you face to face!

VOICE
    You can not see my face until you smell the
    fragrance of the old, old flower.

BOBOLARA
    You can not help until I see your face and I can
    not see your face until I smell the fragrance of
    the old, old flower.

VOICE
    I have nothing more to say. Halloo! Hoola!

BOBOLARA (*mechanically*)
    I know the old, old flower will never bloom; yet
    I shall continue to search and to wait. (*Bobo-
    lara goes out*)

VOICE
    High on the hills
    By lakes and rills
    She'll fly on shadowed wings:
    She'll find the flower
    Within the hour —
    Before the wild bird sings.
    [*Enter the Baron Milton-Maurice.
    He is young, confident and confiding.*

MILTON-MAURICE
    To-day I am one and twenty. To-day I come

to this lonely place to hear the story of my future. Halloo! Hoola!

VOICE
Halloo! Hoola!

MILTON-MAURICE
Are you The Person Passing By?

VOICE
Halloo! Hoola!

MILTON-MAURICE
Mullion! Mizzen!
The moon is risen
And only one star is near:
The mist has spread
From its valley bed —
Oh, Passer, do you hear?

VOICE
Plucky! Plenty!
You're one and twenty,
Is there something you would know?
This is your choice
To hear my voice
Speak truth or naught — or go.

MILTON-MAURICE
Belith! Belath!
I've followed the path
That leads to this lonely place.
For hours — full nine —
I've climbed to the shrine
Where I hope to see your face.

VOICE
You can not see
The face of me
Until a torch burns blue:
One test I make

17

For pity's sake,
For love, for hope, for you.

MILTON-MAURICE

Mullion! Mizzen!
The moon is risen
And only one star is near:
The mist has spread
From its valley bed —
Oh, Passer, I am here.

VOICE

Can you taste?

MILTON-MAURICE

I can taste.

VOICE

What can you taste?

MILTON-MAURICE

On the way I passed a tree where a wondrous
fruit hung low. I ate of it and it had a flavor
like chaff.

VOICE

You can not taste.

MILTON-MAURICE

The taste was like chaff, I say.

VOICE

There was a delicious flavor like the honey from
a forget-me-not.

MILTON-MAURICE

Alas! I can not taste . . . I need your help.

VOICE

I can not help until you see my face.

MILTON-MAURICE

I can not see your face until a torch burns blue.

VOICE

I have nothing more to say. Halloo! Hoola!

MILTON-MAURICE

Oh, Caratina, Caratina, how can we wed? Until I taste we can not live happily ever afterward. I can not learn to taste until I see his face. I can not see his face until a torch burns blue.

[*Enter the Marquess of Strenathco.*

He is a little man with infinite vanity, and the assurance that comes with great wealth.

THE MARQUESS OF STRENATHCO

What is this foolishness?

MILTON-MAURICE

I have come to this lonely place, my Father, to learn how to be happy ever after.

THE MARQUESS OF STRENATHCO

Silly boy, come home and play a game of ninepins with me.

MILTON-MAURICE

No, Father, no. I must first find the torch that's burning blue.

THE MARQUESS OF STRENATHCO

Stuff and nonsense!

MILTON-MAURICE

And then I shall find the Lady Bobolara and ask her for the hand of the lovely Caratina.

THE MARQUESS OF STRENATHCO

What! Marry the grand-daughter of my father's enemy?

MILTON-MAURICE

She is not my enemy. Why should I dislike her because my grandfather disliked her grandfather?

THE MARQUESS OF STRENATHCO

Milton-Maurice, my son, have you no family pride? Give up this mad whim and come home. You can not wed the Lady Caratina.

MILTON-MAURICE

My Father, I am going to live happily ever after!

THE MARQUESS OF STRENATHCO

See how happy I am! I am the richest man in all the world.

MILTON-MAURICE

But you are not happy.

THE MARQUESS OF STRENATHCO

Why?

MILTON-MAURICE

You are not happy because the Lady Bobolara is richer than you are.

THE MARQUESS OF STRENATHCO

For that I can not forgive her! What right has she to be richer than I am?

VOICE

Mildew! Moldew!
Let nothing hold you
From your way, oh, Milton-Maurice
Within the hour
An old, old flower
Will help bring lasting peace.

THE MARQUESS OF STRENATHCO

I think I hear a voice. Who speaks?

MILTON-MAURICE

It is The Person Passing By.

THE MARQUESS OF STRENATHCO

Where is he?

MILTON-MAURICE

No one knows; we seek, and seek to see his face.

THE MARQUESS OF STRENATHCO

What nonsense is this?

VOICE
   Halloo!   Hoola!
THE MARQUESS OF STRENATHCO (*as one who hears through a mist*)
   Who speaks?
VOICE
   Halloo!   Hoola!
THE MARQUESS OF STRENATHCO
   If you are here show me your face.
VOICE
   Belith!   Belath!
   Old man of wrath
   You'll never see my face
   Until you hear
   A bird song clear
   In this moonlit, lonely place.
THE MARQUESS OF STRENATHCO
   What trick is this?
MILTON-MAURICE
   Oh, perfect bliss
   That my father must learn to hear.
THE MARQUESS OF STRENATHCO
   My ears are good
   For any mood
   Except a song of cheer.
VOICE
   Bingle!   Bungle!
   Life's a jungle
   For a stern, old man like you.
   There's just one thing:
   Hear the wild bird sing
   And learn to dance in the dew.
THE MARQUESS OF STRENATHCO
   Dance in the dew!

MILTON-MAURICE
  A man like you!
VOICE
  While the wild bird sings the tune.
THE MARQUESS OF STRENATHCO
  With bitter word
  I'll stone the bird
  By the light of the silver moon.
VOICE
  Ah, you can be
  Like him and me
  If you but use your eyes to see.
THE MARQUESS OF STRENATHCO
  My pride is based
  On a perfect taste,
  And none can smell like me.
MILTON-MAURICE
  But he can't hear
  The bird song clear
  That floats from this lonely place
  Like melodious light
  On a moonlit night —
VOICE
  Then he can not see my face.
THE MARQUESS OF STRENATHCO
  Now why should I
  Wish to descry
  The features of fairy folk?
  You can't engage
  To lessen my age;
  My wrinkles you can't revoke.
VOICE
  Forget your fears,
  Forget the years,

Forget all else but this;
You'll have to hear
The bird-song clear
Or give up all hope of bliss.

THE MARQUESS OF STRENATHCO
I've tried to hear
The bird-song clear,
But the song is harsh, I say —
I hate the notes
From feathered throats,
I hate the trill and roundelay.

VOICE
You'll have to thrill
To the bird-voice trill —
You must learn to love the song;
Else with open eyes
You'll search the skies
But find that all life is wrong.

THE MARQUESS OF STRENATHCO
I can't, I say.

VOICE
Then have your way!
I spake and you will not heed.

THE MARQUESS OF STRENATHCO
The sound I hate.

VOICE
Accept your fate . . .

THE MARQUESS OF STRENATHCO (*after a terrible struggle with his vanity and his assurance*)
O, Passer, your help I need.

MILTON-MAURICE
Father!   *You* ask for help!

VOICE
Kelee!   Keloy!

He asks for joy
He's throttled his silly pride!
When he tastes the fruit
With the succulent root
I'll reveal myself at his side.

MILTON-MAURICE

Bezit! Bezoot!
Please seek the fruit
And learn the charm of laughter —

THE MARQUESS OF STRENATHCO (*eagerly*)

We'll heed the voice
And make the choice —

MILTON-MAURICE

To live happily ever after.

THE MARQUESS OF STRENATHCO

Where is the fruit
With the succulent root?

MILTON-MAURICE

I passed it on the way here.
The land I'll search
Till I find the torch —

THE MARQUESS OF STRENATHCO

Oh, Passer, will you stay here?

MILTON-MAURICE

I'll return to you
With the will to do
And I'll bring the flame that's burning blue.

VOICE

Me-la! Me-lo!

THE MARQUESS OF STRENATHCO

Let's go!

MILTON-MAURICE

Let's go!

24

VOICE

And the search you'll never rue.
[*The Marquess of Strenathco and Milton-Maurice rush out.*

VOICE

O'er hill and hollow
Good luck will follow
And everything's coming out right;
When they return
They'll be ready to learn
A way to see the light.
[*Enter Caratina.*
She carries a wondrous fruit in her hands.

CARATINA (*calling*)

Mother, Mother, I've searched high and low for the bird, but I found only this lovely fruit. Mother!
[*Enter Bobolara.*
Caratina hides the fruit behind her.
Bobolara carries a torch with a blue flame.

BOBOLARA

Woe is me! I have hunted everywhere for the old, old flower, and I found only this torch that burns blue.
[*Enter Milton-Maurice.*
Bobolara hides the torch behind her back.
Milton-Maurice carries a large flower that is closed.

MILTON-MAURICE

I found no torch, but in my path there bloomed a flower. Ah, Caratina — (*He hides the flower behind him*)

BOBOLARA

You can not wed my daughter!

[*All three, and later the Marquess of Stren-*
athco, seem to be in a haze. Everyone is of,
and for himself alone.
Enter the Marquess of Strenathco.
He carries a marvelous bird on his hand.

THE MARQUESS OF STRENATHCO

I could not find the fruit but I have found a
bird: he is mute.

BOBOLARA (*to Milton-Maurice*)

You can not wed my daughter!

THE MARQUESS OF STRENATHCO (*hiding the bird*
behind him)

What?

BOBOLARA

Caratina, tell Milton-Maurice that I did not
address his father.

THE MARQUESS OF STRENATHCO

My son can not wed your daughter? Indeed
he can *not* wed your daughter!

VOICE

Hush! End this strife
As you love life
And try to live in peace:
Just look about
And you'll find out
That wonders never cease!

CARATINA

What does he mean?

BOBOLARA

There is no meaning. For nine and thirty
years he has promised something, but I can not
see any hope.

VOICE
> Look down! look up!
> The bitter cup
> Is almost drained to the leas;
> Let each one try
> To face the sky
> And see what each one sees. (*With strange obedience all four face the sky*)

THE MARQUESS OF STRENATHCO
> Yon tall, tall tree touches the nearest star!

BOBOLARA
> Absurd!

VOICE
> Oh, clouds and rifts —
> You all bear gifts
> That you hide behind your backs;
> Put out your hands
> To my commands
> Or shiver and shake in your tracks.
> [*They put out their hands, each one disclosing what another has sought.*

BOBOLARA
> I smell the breath of an old, old flower — Oh, Passer, are you here?

MILTON-MAURICE
> I see the blue of a burning torch — Oh, Passer, are you here?

THE MARQUESS OF STRENATHCO
> I taste the fruit with the succulent root — Oh, Passer, are you here?

CARATINA
> I hear the song the wild bird sings — Oh, Passer, are you here?

[*The light begins to fade from the world and strange music fills the air.*

VOICE
From North and South
From source and mouth
I come through the worlds to you —
From East and West,
From vale and crest,
I'm bringing a message true.
River and brook
Learn to look
At persons passing by —
Oh, use your ears
And use your tears
For a person passing by.
[*There is a long, still blackness and when the light again appears The Person Passing By is seen beside the four.*

BOBOLARA (*fearfully*)
Caratina, is he there? I dare not look.

CARATINA (*in wonder. To her he seems calm and tender and strong*)
He is there!
[*They all look.*

BOBOLARA
Why, he is like any other man.

THE PERSON PASSING BY
You see that, and yet you can not see yon tall, tall tree touch on the nearest star!

THE MARQUESS OF STRENATHCO
This man has played a trick on us. (*To the Marquess of Strenathco, too, he is like any other man*)

28

THE PERSON PASSING BY
  When I could not be seen you listened to me and
  feared me.   Now that I am here you doubt me.
THE MARQUESS OF STRENATHCO
  I doubt you, but I shall be fair to you.   I shall
  test you.
  [*A faint, golden light illumines the face of The
  Person Passing By.*
MILTON-MAURICE
  Father!   Father!
THE MARQUESS OF STRENATHCO
  I shall test him!   (*Age has seen wonder so
  long that even wonder is a commonplace*)
CARATINA
  What shall we do to live happily ever after?
  [*The Person Passing By smiles gently at Cara-
  tina.   The smile seems to awaken a strange
  tenderness in Bobolara.*
BOBOLARA
  I have so little time to live.   Tell me how to be
  happy.
  [*The Person Passing By smiles gently at her
  and at Milton-Maurice and pityingly at the
  Marquess of Strenathco.*
THE PERSON PASSING BY
  You do not understand.
  (*To Caratina*)
  You can not smell a pleasant fragrance;
  (*To Milton-Maurice*)
  You can not taste a delicate flavor;
  (*To Bobolara*)
  You can not see a glorious sight;
  (*To the Marquess of Strenathco*)
  You can not hear a lovely sound.

29

There is a shadow over your eyes.
And over your tongue,
And over your nose,
And over your ears.
Your defects are all different; and yet to live happily ever after, you and all the world need the same thing.

ALL
And what do we need?

THE PERSON PASSING BY
You need a trimplet.

THE MARQUESS OF STRENATHCO (*remembering his importance*)
Oh, yes, I never thought of that.

THE PERSON PASSING BY
You know what a trimplet is then?

THE MARQUESS OF STRENATHCO
Do you?

THE PERSON PASSING BY
Do you know what a trimplet is?

THE MARQUESS OF STRENATHCO
I know if you know.

THE PERSON PASSING BY
Perhaps you do — then you'll tell the rest; I'll stand your test. Remember in a trimplet lies all happiness.

CARATINA
Are there enough trimplets for all of us?

THE PERSON PASSING BY
One trimplet is enough for all of you.

CARATINA
Where is the trimplet?

THE PERSON PASSING BY
It might be here, or there, or anywhere; but

THE TRIMPLET

sometimes you have to have patience and wait.

BOBOLARA
Patience and wait! I have waited nine and thirty years!
[*The golden light on the face of The Person Passing By has become stronger until it has become an overpowering radiance.*

THE PERSON PASSING BY
You have been stubborn and impatient.

BOBOLARA
Stubborn and impatient! My life is almost at an end. I must hurry.

THE PERSON PASSING BY
Why hurry? — Heaven is full of days and they are all coming this way.

BOBOLARA
They are nearly all gone for me.

THE PERSON PASSING BY
There will always be more and more and more to come.
[*The Person Passing By moves, as if to go.*

THE MARQUESS OF STRENATHCO
The trimplet! I can't remember its color.

THE PERSON PASSING BY
Well, I'll tell you this: — a trimplet can rest in your hand but you can not hold it. It can lie upon your fingers but it can not hold them. Good-bye. I'm passing on. Halloo! Hoola!
[*The Person Passing By has disappeared in the gathered gloom. . . . It brightens.*

BOBOLARA
What is a trimplet?

THE MARQUESS OF STRENATHCO
She speaks to me for the first time in nine and thirty years.
[*A man of affairs does not always speak to the point.*

BOBOLARA
What is a trimplet?

THE MARQUESS OF STRENATIICO
Why it's a —

BOBOLARA
What is it?   Speak!

THE MARQUESS OF STRENATHCO
I can not remember its color.

BOBOLARA
What is it?

THE MARQUESS OF STRENATHCO
Woman, I do not know!

ALL
What!   You do not know?

THE MARQUESS OF STRENATHCO
I couldn't tell him I didn't know.   He would think me a fool.

CARATINA
Oh, and I can not live happily ever after.

BOBOLARA
Madman!

MILTON-MAURICE
Have patience, I shall ask.   Halloo!   Hoola!

VOICE
I have nothing more to say.   Halloo!   Hoola!

MILTON-MAURICE
I want to ask just one question.

BOBOLARA
One question only.

VOICE
  Halloo! Hoola!
CARATINA
  Please! Please! To-day I am one and
  twenty!
VOICE
  Halloo! Hoola!
  [*The Marquess of Strenathco has been search-
  ing for something.*
THE MARQUESS OF STRENATHCO
  Come back! Come back!
VOICE
  Halloo! Hoola! (*He laughs a laugh that
  seems to roll through the skies*)
BOBOLARA
  Now you've done it! You — with your pride
  and your deafness!
MILTON-MAURICE
  Well, there's only one thing to do: hunt for the
  trimplet.
CARATINA
  I know it isn't this torch.
VOICE
  Halloo! Hoola!
MILTON-MAURICE
  It isn't this wild bird song.
VOICE
  Halloo! Hoola!
THE MARQUESS OF STRENATHCO
  I wish I knew its color.
BOBOLARA
  Stupid! That wouldn't help. Everything
  here is gloom.
  [*The ray of golden light appears again.*

33

CARATINA
  What is that golden light?

MILTON-MAURICE
  Perhaps a sunbeam has slipped through the moon.

VOICE
  Halloo! Hoola!

BOBOLARA
  I have hunted everywhere.

MILTON-MAURICE
  Let's sit down and think.
  [*They all sit down and think. They are a ludicrous lot.*

THE MARQUESS OF STRENATHCO
  We might as well give up.

BOBOLARA
  No, I have been face to face with The Person Passing By. I shall stay here to the end.

YOU (*in the audience*)
  Why don't you look out here?

THE MARQUESS OF STRENATHCO
  Who are you, sir?

YOU
  I live in nowadays; but I think I can help you find the trimplet.

BOBOLARA
  Impertinent!

CARATINA
  He might as well try, Mother dear.

MILTON-MAURICE
  He can't do worse than fail.

THE MARQUESS OF STRENATHCO
  All right, we're coming.

THE TRIMPLET

YOU
It can't be this handkerchief — no, for I can hold that.

CARATINA (*now in the audience*)
It's not this flower.

THE MARQUESS OF STRENATHCO (*now in the audience*)
Perhaps it's the light of this little girl's eyes.

BOBOLARA
Look under the chair.

MILTON-MAURICE (*far out in the audience*)
It's not up here.

BOBOLARA (*to You*)
See, you silly person, you have dragged us into nowadays to no purpose.

THE MARQUESS OF STRENATHCO
I'm going back.

YOU
I'll go with you.

ALL
What?

YOU
Perhaps I can find it up there.

THE MARQUESS OF STRENATHCO
You could find where we had failed. Ha! Ha!

YOU
I'm going anyway.
[*You starts for the stage, but Milton-Maurice intercepts him.*

MILTON-MAURICE
Well, promise if you come into the play you won't wed the lovely Caratina.

YOU

I don't want to wed any one yet. I want to find the trimplet.

[*You runs on to the stage followed by the others. The ray of golden light falls upon his hand. He tests it. It rests in his hand but he can not hold it. It lies upon his fingers but it can not hold them.*

YOU (*triumphantly*)

The trimplet! I know what a trimplet is!

THE MARQUESS OF STRENATHCO

What is it?

YOU

A trimplet is the hole a sunbeam makes in a shadow.

VOICE

Halloo! Hoola!
A light — a light
Shines in the night
And fills their souls with splendor!

STRENATHCO

How can a trimplet cure my deafness?

VOICE

Move to the right,
Stand in the light,
And fill your souls with splendor.

[*Caratina walks with mingled hope and fear to the right of the golden ray and then steps into the light. Bobolara follows, then Milton-Maurice, then Strenathco. Each is affected to the depths of his soul as The Person Passing By speaks the word that restores his lost sense.*

VOICE

Smell . . . See . . . Taste . . . Hear . . .

36

[*As he commands the inanimate things obey.
The trees sigh, the torch glows, the flower opens
and the bird sings.*

Blow . . . Glow . . . Burst . . . Sing . . .

[*Then with the triumph of all the world —*
Love is far — love is near —
Love is everything.

THE MARQUESS OF STRENATHCO

I hear the wild bird's song.

CARATINA

I smell the fragrance of a thousand trees.

MILTON-MAURICE

I taste the flavor of the honey of forget-me-
nots.

BOBOLARA

I see yon tall, tall tree touch on the nearest
star! (*then to the Marquess of Strenathco*)
Neighbor, Heaven has sent a new day.

[*There is a pause.*
*Then You, who has stepped aside and
watched the play with breathless interest, now
takes a hand.*

YOU (*to Caratina and Milton-Maurice*)

Now, you two must wed and live happily ever
after . . . If you don't I won't like the play
very much.   I'm not sure that I like it anyway,
because heaven knows how long it would have
kept up if I hadn't helped you find the trimplet.

VOICE

The play's near done
And every one
Has learned a simple lesson.

YOU

I don't think it fair to try to teach us a lesson

every time you tell us a story. I like a play
that is a play. If this had been a good play —
I couldn't have got into it.
(*To the audience*) Could I?

THE MARQUESS OF STRENATHCO

Well, we did our very best and I think it's a
pretty good play, and so does the author.
Now you go on out there. The play isn't
ended yet.

YOU

It must have a pretty ending, mind you.

[*You returns to his seat.*

THE MARQUESS OF STRENATHCO

Caratina, here is the hand of my son, the Baron
Milton-Maurice.

[*He turns to You for approval.*

YOU (*approving but adding a final touch*)

You must give him a dowry.

THE MARQUESS OF STRENATHCO

I give him all my land that lies between the ends
of the rainbow.

[*A rainbow forms in the sky.*

VOICE

In the valley, you
Will dance in the dew
While the wild bird sings the tune.
For what is so rare
As a rainbow there
Afloat in the light of the moon?
To help the tale
He gives a vale
That to the rainbow bends,
And we are told
That pots of gold

38

Lie at the rainbow ends.

YOU (*after waiting a moment for the complete conclusion of the story*)

You ought to say something, Babalora.

THE MARQUESS OF STRENATHCO

Her name is not Babalora — it's Bobolara.

BOBOLARA

Well, we've certainly worked hard enough for you to know our names at least.

CARATINA

But he's quite right, Mother; you ought to say something.

YOU

Yes, you ought to say something — whether we know your name or not.

BOBOLARA

Quite right, I ought. I shall give to Caratina the castle of jade in the garden where the gold flowers blow. (*To Caratina*) And you shall live there happily ever after.

YOU (*satisfied*)

For Heaven is full of days and they're all coming this way!

VOICE

Warm sun, blue sky,
If you only try
You'll be a person passing by,
Who knows the why
Of the sibilant sigh —
Oh, for a person passing by!
Halloo! Hoola!
Halloo! Hoola!

(*The Curtains Close*)

NEVERTHELESS

A Girl
A Boy
A Burglar

The Scene is a room just upstairs.
The Time is last night — or to-night, perhaps.

PROLOGUE
Our next play is an interlude before the curtains. You may sleep during an interlude, but
you mustn't snore or have the nightmare because that would be very discourteous to the
author and very discouraging to us. We can
not live if you do not like us, and you can not
like us if you do not keep awake.

[*After the Prologue has bowed the Device-
Bearer brings two chairs, a stool, a table, a lamp
and places them on the forestage. If you are
not a very grown-up you know immediately that
you are in a room that belongs to very young
people.*

[*The Boy enters carrying a book. He is angry.
He looks around to see if any one is looking and
then goes to the table and tries to remove some
money from a small bank that has two locks;
but he can't find the keys.*
[*As he is shaking it violently in an attempt to
force it, the Girl enters.*

GIRL
Billie!

BOY
I will force it!

GIRL
You made a compact with me.

43

BOY

Don't use words like that — I hate words.
(*He continues to try to force the bank*)

GIRL

It's a miserable shame, Billie Cleves!

BOY

Now, Lou, don't use any more words on me.
I won't stand it.

GIRL

Well, what shall I say?

BOY

Say *dirty* shame.

GIRL

Billie!

BOY

I don't care. I'm tired of being corrected all
the time. When I'm old enough to paddle my
own canoe, I'm going to murder grammar all
the time. I'm going to use short words and I
hope I'll say I seen and I would have went.

GIRL

Billie Cleves!

BOY

And, if I can get this bank open, I'll go away
forever to-night and I'll talk just as I please.

GIRL

My, Billie! You *are* angry!

BOY

Angry! I'm mad! I'm awful mad! (*He
shakes the bank terrifically*)

GIRL

You'll break it.

BOY

I don't care. I'm going to bust it —

44

GIRL
Billie, Mother wouldn't like that word at all.
BOY
I don't care.   I'm going to bu — break it open
and then I'm going to leave home for-
ever.
(*He puts it on the floor and starts to trample
it*)
GIRL
Billie Cleves, don't you dare!   That's half
mine.   And you can't open it unless we both
agree.
BOY
Who said so?
GIRL
Why, it was our compact.
BOY
If you were fourteen years old, Louise Cleves,
and your mother punished you for speaking bad
English you'd forget all about compacts.
GIRL
No, I wouldn't.
BOY
Yes, you would.
GIRL
No, I wouldn't.
BOY
You don't know what you'd do; you're not four-
teen and you're not a boy.
GIRL
I wouldn't break a compact if I were a hundred
and fourteen.
BOY
Now, Lou, listen.

45

GIRL

I don't want to listen.

BOY

Just put yourself in my place.

GIRL

Billie Cleves, we agreed never, never to open
that bank until we were in need of food and
clothing.

BOY

Well, I'm in need, Lou.

GIRL

No, you're not; Father and Mother give you
all the food and clothes you want.

BOY

But I'm going to run away forever and go to
Honolulu or Texas.

GIRL

No, you're not.

BOY

I am.

GIRL

Well, Billie, you deserved to be corrected.

BOY

All I said was, " Jim's a rotten rider."   And he
is.

GIRL

Well, that wasn't nice.

BOY (*exasperated at not being able to open the
bank*)

Lou, where is my key?

GIRL

I put it away.

BOY

Where?

GIRL
Our compact was for me to take the key to your blue lock and hide it, and you were to take the key to my pink lock and hide it so we couldn't fall into temptation.

BOY
I'll pick the locks like a burglar.

GIRL
You can't. They're both pick-proof. And there's only one key in all the whole wide world for each lock.

BOY
I'll get your key and open your lock.

GIRL
My key won't open your lock.

BOY
I can't find yours where I hid it.

GIRL
I found it and hid it again.

BOY
Where is it?

GIRL
I don't think I ought to tell you, Billie, I'm afraid you'll fall into temptation.

BOY
How about you?

GIRL
Boys are more easily tempted than women.

BOY
H-m!

GIRL
Because they get out more.

BOY
I'll throw it and break it.

GIRL

Now, Billie, don't be rash.

BOY

I don't care.

GIRL

Father'll hear you.

BOY

Father won't hear me much longer about this house.

GIRL

Please, Billie, read your book.

BOY

I won't do it, I won't.   I'm sick of goody-goody books.

GIRL

What did mother give you to read?

BOY (*sullenly*)

There it is.

GIRL

"The Narrow Path!"   Why, she sent me up here to read that, too.

BOY

What for?

GIRL

I said " he don't " instead of " he doesn't."

BOY

Just after I said it?

GIRL

Yes.

BOY

You *are* a goose.

GIRL

But I don't get angry like you do.

BOY

You're not as old as I am. Other boys of my age do pretty much as they please.

GIRL

Well, here we are.   There's no use quarrelling, because it's mother's plan to make us read a fine book whenever we make mistakes in grammar. And you know mother's plans! (*She opens the book*) Oh, dear, no pictures! . . . Let's hurry up.

BOY

I won't do it.

GIRL

Come on, Billie, and get it over with.

BOY

Give me the keys or I'll break — I'll *bust* it.

GIRL

I won't give you the keys and you won't break it — William Cleves, if you don't live up to our compact, I'll not have anything more to do with you.

BOY

I don't care.   (*He throws the bank violently*)

GIRL

Billie! (*She pounces upon the bank and bursts into tears*)

GIRL

I never thought you'd do it.

[*The Boy moves about uneasily.*

I never thought you'd do it. (*She weeps torrentially*)

BOY

Now, Lou —

49

GIRL

You broke our compact and tried to destroy our bank.

BOY (*defiantly*)

I tried to *bust* it — and I hope I did.

GIRL

Billie Cleves! — Well, you didn't even nick it. (*She takes up the book after carefully placing the bank so that the Boy can't get it*)

BOY

Lou, won't you lend me the keys a moment?

GIRL (*relentlessly*)

You broke a compact.

BOY

Please, Lou.

GIRL

I have my reading to do.

BOY

I'm going to go away — forever — Lou!

GIRL

Good-bye.

BOY (*fiercely*)

I want my money!

GIRL

It's *our* money.   And I'm the guardian.

BOY

All right. . . . Good-bye.

GIRL

Good-bye. (*Reading*)   " The Narrow Path is very steep and straight.   It leads to a land of gold and it is not easy to negotiate because Heaven thinks it is best for people to climb for what they want.   Nevertheless —"

BOY

Are you going to give me the money to run away with?

GIRL

No.

BOY

Good-bye.

GIRL

A compact is binding to both parties, father says.

BOY

Good-bye.

GIRL

Good-bye. (*Reading*) Nevertheless — nevertheless — (*She begins to giggle deliciously*)

BOY

What's funny, Lou?

GIRL

Come here and look, Billie.
[*The Boy drags himself to the book.*

BOY

What?

GIRL

This word.

BOY

Never — the — less. It's just like any other word.

GIRL

No, it isn't. *Steep* and *straight* and *the* all look like something. But this is just funny.

BOY

Nevertheless.
[*The Girl goes off into gales of laughter.*

BOY. (*Reading further and turning the page*)
Here it is again. (*He laughs*)

GIRL
Where?

BOY
Here. (*Turning back*)

GIRL
Neverthe —(*turning the page and going into another paroxysm of laughter as she finds the rest of the word on the next page*)— less.

BOY
It *is* funny-looking!

GIRL
What does it mean?

BOY
I'll look in the dictionary.

GIRL
I know what it means in a way, but I can't explain it —

BOY
So do I. (*He goes to the dictionary*)

GIRL
Never — the — less. (*She looks up and sees that the Boy is busy. She looks around cautiously, then takes up the bank and hides it. As she hears the Boy coming back, she resumes her seat and the book*)

BOY
It means *notwithstanding, yet, however*. . . .

GIRL
Dictionaries never tell you the real, honest, true, live meaning, do they, Billie?

BOY (*fascinated*)
Never — the — less.

52

"Nevertheless"

The Girl and Boy encounter a strange word

GIRL

It's three words all huddled together. (*She pictures it on her fingers*)

BOY (*counting the words on his fingers*)

Never — the — less.

GIRL

How did they come together?

BOY (*losing himself in the puzzle*)

I don't know.

GIRL

Let's ask mother.

BOY (*remembering his anger*)

No, I won't.

GIRL

I will.

BOY

Let's be independent, Lou. I don't like to ask favors when I'm punished.

GIRL

Well, I'm being punished, too; but I want to know all about this funny word.

BOY

Let's try some other way.

GIRL

I know!

BOY

What?

GIRL

They say if you put out the lights and shut your eyes very tight and wait very patiently that an elf will come and tell you anything you want to know.

BOY

I don't believe in elfs.

GIRL

Billie!

BOY

I don't.

GIRL

The plural of elf is elves.   We had it to-day.

BOY (*exasperated*)

I knew it,— but I get tired of having to think about everything before I speak.   Sometimes I try not to think at all.

GIRL (*going to the lamp*)

I'm going to turn out the light.

BOY (*scornfully*)

Nothing will happen.

GIRL

Well, we can try.

BOY (*hunting*)

Lou, where's the bank?

GIRL

I hid it, Billie.

BOY

You shan't hide my money!

GIRL

Keep quiet, Billie, and sit down.   (*She puts the light out*)

BOY (*sheepishly*)

I feel so silly.

GIRL

Are your eyes shut?

BOY

No.

GIRL

Billy, please shut your eyes.

54

BOY
   I won't do it . . . I'm going to turn on the
   light.
GIRL
   Now, Billie . . .
   [*He evidently starts for the lamp.*
   I'll give you the keys if you're good.
BOY
   Now?
GIRL
   No, afterward.
BOY (*turning on the lamp*)
   Promise.
GIRL
   Yes.   (*Out goes the light as she pulls it*)   Are
   you sitting down?
BOY
   Uh-huh!
GIRL
   Are your eyes shut?
BOY
   Uh-huh!
GIRL
   Tight?
BOY
   Uh-huh!
GIRL
   And when he comes don't talk.
BOY
   Uh —.
GIRL
   'Cause you don't believe and you might frighten
   him away.

BOY
Uh —.
GIRL
Where are you, Billie?
BOY
Here I am.
GIRL
Move over.
BOY
There isn't much room.
GIRL
Now. (*Silence*) Do you hear anything?
BOY
No.
[*Silence.*
A pale light appears between the curtains, then a dark form.
The light is shut off and presently reappears at the table.
The Burglar opens the drawers and, taking out some pretty things, puts them in his pocket. The light goes out.
Silence.
GIRL
Billie, I just can't stand it a moment longer. Don't you hear the elf? . . . (*A sound*) There he is!
[*The light comes on again and the Burglar takes up the bank. Just as he is putting it in his pocket, the Girl speaks.*
GIRL
Do you know what *nevertheless* means?
[*The bank goes clattering to the floor.*
The light is turned upon the two children. *The*
56

Burglar takes a step forward and stumbles over the bank.

BURGLAR

Don't holler.

[*The Boy turns the light on.*

BOY

A burglar!

GIRL

If you don't move, Billie, a burglar won't hurt you.

BOY

Hold up your hands, Lou.

BOY and GIRL (*holding their hands up*)

We give up.

BURGLAR

Put out the light.

GIRL

Please don't put out the light . . . We'll be good.

[*A door is heard to close in the next room.*

BURGLAR

Put out the light. (*The light goes out*) Who was that?

GIRL

Mary.

BURGLAR

What's she doing?

BOY

Don't you tell him, Lou. Make him let you turn the light on.

GIRL (*deciding to weep*)

I'm afraid of the dark.

BURGLAR

Quit your bawling and put on the light.

[*The Boy puts on the light.*
What's she doing?
GIRL
She's setting the burglar alarm for the night.
BURGLAR
How do I get out of here?
GIRL
You can't get out because if you open anything all the bells will ring and the police will come.
BOY (*bravely stepping forward*)
We'll put you in jail. (*As the Burglar turns, however, he wilts*)
GIRL
Billie, let's let him go if he tells us what nevertheless means.
BURGLAR
Huh?
GIRL
Do you know what nevertheless means?
BURGLAR
What's nevertheless?
GIRL
It's a word.
BURGLAR
What's the game?
BOY
If you know what nevertheless means we'll let you go.
GIRL
It's a compact.
BURGLAR
Promise you won't give me up.
GIRL
We won't give you up . . . Sit down.

[*The Burglar sits.*

BOY

Where's your pistol?

BURGLAR

I ain't got none.

GIRL

Oh, you mustn't say that.

BURGLAR

Well, I ain't.

GIRL

It's very wrong to say " I ain't." My mother would make us read *all* " The Narrow Path " if we talked like that.

BURGLAR (*puzzled*)

What!

BOY

They carry pistols in Texas.

BURGLAR

Well, I ain't never used none, and I ain't never been in Texas, and what's more I ain't never going to Texas!

GIRL

He's a very pleasant burglar, Billie.

BURGLAR

Well, I'm in a pickle, but I can't hurt no kids.

GIRL

See, Billie, how bad grammar sounds.

BURGLAR

I don't care nothing about grammar. When you have to paddle your own canoe, you can't take no time for grammar.

GIRL

Oh, dear Billie, don't ever paddle your own canoe . . . Billie . . . (*She goes to whisper to*

the Boy) (*To the Burglar, as she passes him*)
Excuse me. (*To the Boy*) I'm going to try
Mother's plan on him. I'm going to read to
him!

[*The Burglar rises and looks around.*

BOY (*whispering*)

I'm going to call father.

GIRL

Now, Billie, maybe we can make him good.

BOY

Well, he can't get away and he hasn't a pistol —

BURGLAR

Hey, quit your jawing and give me up if you
want to.

GIRL

We're not going to give you up.

BURGLAR

Huh?

GIRL

We're going to read to you.

BURGLAR

Quit your kidding.

GIRL

How does it feel to be a burglar?

BURGLAR

Not so good.

GIRL

Aren't you afraid to be a burglar?

BOY

'Course not. Look how big he is.

GIRL

Aren't you ashamed to be a burglar?

BURGLAR

Well . . . I ain't never burgled before.

GIRL

Well, that's not so bad, *but* just the same we're going to read to you.

BURGLAR

What for?

GIRL

Because you use bad grammar.

BURGLAR

You're funny kids.   Ain't you scared?

BOY (*magnificently*)

No!

BURGLAR (*turning suddenly*)

Huh?

[*The Boy retreats ingloriously.*

GIRL

You wouldn't hurt us, would you?

BURGLAR

Why wouldn't I?

GIRL

We didn't do anything to you.

BURGLAR

You trapped me.

GIRL

We didn't know you were coming.

BURGLAR

What was you hiding for?

GIRL

We expected someone else.

BURGLAR

Go on!

[*The Boy moves a chair cautiously toward the Burglar and finally summons the courage to sit down beside him.*

BOY (*pleasantly*)

Did you know Jessie James?

BURGLAR

I heard of him but I ain't never seen him.

GIRL

What made you begin?

BURGLAR

Never mind . . . I began and I got caught.
. . . Now what?

GIRL

I'm going to read to you.

BURGLAR (*resignedly*)

Go ahead.

GIRL

Do you want to read, Billie?

BOY (*unselfishly*)

No!

GIRL

This is all about the narrow path.

BURGLAR

Uh-huh.

GIRL (*reading*)

" The Narrow Path is very steep and straight.
It leads to a land of gold and it is not easy to
negotiate because Heaven thinks it is best for
people to climb for what they want. Nevertheless —"

[*The Boy and Girl burst out laughing so suddenly that the Burglar is quite startled.*

BURGLAR (*uneasily*)

What are you laughing at?

GIRL (*pointing to " nevertheless "*)

It's such a funny word.

BURGLAR

Ain't it just like other words?

GIRL

Don't it look funny?

BOY

Don't it look funny?

GIRL

I mean doesn't it look funny?

[*The three huddle together over the book.*

BURGLAR (*muttering*)

N-E-V-E-R-T-H-E-L-E-S-S.   Huh!   It does look sort o' funny . . . What's the rest of it?

GIRL (*reading*)

" Nevertheless the narrow path is not all hardship."

BURGLAR

Maybe not; but it was pretty hard for me.

GIRL

Have you tried it?

BURGLAR

Yep.   But I slipped. . . . Go on.

GIRL (*reading*)

" On the other hand, the primrose path is broad and it slopes gently downward, but it leads to the land of thorns.   Neverthe —(*She turns a page*)— less —"

[*Again the children go into gales of laughter.*

BURGLAR

Huh?

GIRL

Look.

[*Again they huddle over the book.*

BURGLAR

N-E-V-E-R-T-H-E-L-E-S-S. . . . It *is* funny.

(He joins heartily in the laughter)

GIRL

You see — it's three words and they don't mean anything unless they are all huddled together just like we are now.

[*They all laugh uproariously.*

BOY (*on the friendliest of terms now*)

Do you walk the primrose path?

BURGLAR

Go on! I'm in the land of thorns.

GIRL

Well, how did you get there if you didn't walk the primrose path?

BURGLAR

I just naturally fell.

GIRL

Don't you know the meaning of nevertheless?

BURGLAR

I sort o' know the meaning, but I can't put it into words.

GIRL

Can you act it out?

BURGLAR

Huh?

GIRL

Can you act it out?

BURGLAR

What do you mean — act it out?

GIRL

Sometimes when Billie and I can't put things into words we act it out. Like this: If I want to tell someone what *revolves* means, I just do this . . . and then they know.

BURGLAR

Aw, yes, you pertend!

GIRL

Oh . . . Well — Can't you p-p-pertend never-theless?

BURGLAR

I hardly think so.

BOY

Did you get tired on the narrow path?

BURGLAR

Ye-eh . . . But I wish I hadn't.

GIRL

Can't you climb back?

BURGLAR

Nope.   It's too late.

GIRL

Mother says it's never too late to do right.

BURGLAR

Sure it is.   A man what's been in jail can't get straight again.

BOY (*admiringly*)

Have you been in jail?

BURGLAR

No, but once is enough.

GIRL

When are you going to jail?

BURGLAR

To-night, I guess.

BOY

What for?

BURGLAR

For breaking in here!

GIRL

We aren't going to send you to jail.

BURGLAR

Maybe not, but your paw and maw will. (*Whimsically*) 'Sides I can't tell you what nevertheless means and I can't act it out. And a compact's a compact, ain't it?

GIRL

Mother won't put you in jail. She's too kind.

BOY (*with sad memories*)

But she's awful strict about grammar and ugly words.

GIRL

She says it's easy to walk the narrow path.

BOY

Father isn't so sure, but he says it *can* be done.

GIRL

Come on and we'll help you.

BURGLAR

Come on where?

BOY

Come on and walk the narrow path with us.

BURGLAR

Where is it?

GIRL

Here.

BURGLAR

What's the game?

GIRL

Mother says if we can walk a straight line out that door without wobbling, we can walk the narrow path all our lives without any trouble.

BOY

To speak of.

BURGLAR

What's on the other side of that door?

66

BOY and GIRL
  Father and mother.
BURGLAR
  You seem to be pretty straight kids, but it's too
  late for me.
GIRL
  No, it isn't.
BURGLAR
  Yes, it's too late. I'll take the back door and
  try to make my get-away.
GIRL
  Billie, you ask him.
BOY
  I'd like to have you come with us, sir.
  Dad's a fine man and mother's a great
  woman.
GIRL
  All we have to do is to walk straight through
  that door without wobbling —
BOY
  Come on —
BURGLAR
  I think it's too late for me — nevertheless —
  (*He takes their hands*)
GIRL (*ecstatically*)
  Oh, he's acted out nevertheless! Billie, don't
  you see the real, honest, true, live meaning?
  . . . Come on, let's start.
  [*They start carefully for the door and, as they
  come to the safe they stop. The Burglar looks
  ruefully at it a moment.*
GIRL
  Don't wobble now. We've almost made it—
  [*They keep on for the door.*

Isn't it easy?   And mother says if you can do this little bit, you can do it always.
[*When they disappear through the door, the play is over.*

THE MEDICINE SHOW

Lut'er
Giz
Dr. Stev'n Vandexter

The scene is on the south bank of the Ohio
River. An old soap box, a log and a large stone
are visible. The river is supposed to flow between
the stage and the audience. In the background,
at the top of the " grade " is the village of Rock
Springs.

This is only a quarter of a play.   Its faults are many.   Come, glory in them with us.

You are a little boy once more lying on your rounded belly on the cool, damp sands beside the beautiful river.   You are still young enough to see the wonder that everywhere touches the world; and men are in the world — all sorts of men.   But you can still look upon them with the shining eyes of brotherhood.   You can still feel the mystery that is true understanding. Everywhere about you men and things are reaching for the infinite, each in his own way, be it big or little, be it the moon or a medicine show; and you yourself are not yet decided whether to reach for the stars or go a-fishing. Brother!

[*Lut'er enters or rather oozes in.*
He is a tall, expressionless, uncoordinated per-son who might be called filthy were it not for the fact that the dirt on his skin and on his clothes seems an inherent part of him. *He has a wan smile that — what there is of it — is not displeasing.   Strangely enough, his face is al-ways smooth-shaven.   He carries a fishing pole made from a tree twig and equipped with a thread knotted frequently and a bent pin for hook.*
Lut'er looks about and his eyes light on the
71

*stone. He attempts to move it with his bare
foot to the water's edge, but it is too heavy for
him. Next he looks at the log, raises his foot
to move it, then abandons the attempt because
his eyes rest on the lighter soap box. This he
puts in position never deigning to touch it with
his hands. Then he sits calmly and drawing a
fishing worm from the pocket of his shirt fastens
it on the pin-hook and casts his line into the
water. Thereafter he takes no apparent interest in fishing.*

After a moment Giz enters.

*Giz is somewhat dirtier than Lut'er but the dirt
is less assimilated and consequently less to be
condoned. Besides he is fuzzy with a beard of
long standing. He may have been shaved some
Saturdays ago — but quite ago.*

*Giz doesn't speak to Lut'er and Lut'er doesn't
speak to Giz, but Lut'er suggests life by con-
tinued chewing and he acknowledges the prox-
imity of Giz by spitting and wiping his lips with
his hand. Giz having tried the log and the rock
finally chooses the rock and acknowledges
Lut'er's salivary greeting by spitting also; but
he wipes his mouth on his sleeve.*

*After a moment he reaches forward with his
bare foot and touches the water.*

GIZ

'T's warm as fresh milk.

[*Lut'er, not to be wholly unresponsive, spits.
A fresh silence falls upon them.*

GIZ

'S *Hattie Brown* came in?

72

[*Lut'er spits and almost shakes his head negatively*].
She's a mighty good little steam-boat.

LUT'ER
She's water-logged.

GIZ
She ain't water-logged.

LUT'ER
She is.

GIZ
She ain't.

LUT'ER
She is.

GIZ
She ain't. (*The argument dies of malnutrition. After a moment of silence Giz speaks*)

GIZ
'S river raisin'?

LUT'ER
Nup!
[*Silence*.

GIZ
Fallin'?

LUT'ER
Nup!

GIZ
Standin' still?

LUT'ER
Uh!
[*The conversation might continue if Giz did not catch a mosquito on his leg*.

GIZ
Gosh! A galler-nipper at noon day!

73

[Lut'er scratches back of his ear warily.

GIZ

An' look at the whelp!

[Giz scratches actively, examines the wound and anoints it with tobacco juice.

The Play would be ended at this moment for lack of varied action if Dr. Stev'n Vandexter did not enter.

He is an eager, healthy-looking man with a whitish beard that long washing in Ohio River water has turned yellowish. He wears spectacles and his clothes and general appearance are somewhat an improvement upon Lut'er and Giz. Furthermore he wears what were shoes and both supports of his suspenders are fairly intact. He is whittling a piece of white pine with a large jack-knife.

Seeing Lut'er and Giz he draws the log between them and sits.

After a moment in which three cuds are audibly chewed, Dr. Stev'n speaks.

DOCTOR

What gits me is how they done it.

[For the first time Lut'er turns his head as admission that some one is there.

Giz looks up with a dawn of interest under his beard.

Silence.

DOCTOR

I traded a two pound catfish for a box of that salve: an' I don't see how they done it.

[Lut'er having turned his head keeps it turned. Evidently Dr. Stev'n always has something of interest to say.

74

GIZ

Kickapoo?

DOCTOR

Ye'. Kickapoo Indian Salve. I don't think no Indian never seen it. (*He looks at Giz for acquiescence*)

GIZ

Y'ain't never sure about nothin' these days.

[*Dr. Stev'n looks at Lut'er for acquiescence also, and Lut'er approving turns his head forward and spits assent.*

DOCTOR

I smelled it an' it smelled like ker'sene. I biled it an' it biled over an' burnt up like ker'sene. . . . I don't think it was nothin' but ker'sene an' lard.

GIZ

Reckon 't wuz common ker'sene?

DOCTOR

I don't know whether 't wuz common ker'sene but I know 't wuz ker'sene. . . . An' I bet ker'sene'll cure heaps o' troubles if yer use it right.

GIZ

That air doctor said the salve ud cure most anything.

LUT'ER (*as though a voice from the grave, long forgotten*)

Which doctor?

GIZ

The man doctor — him with the p'inted musstash.

LUT'ER

I seen him take a egg outer Jimmie Weldon's

ear — an' Jimmie swore he didn't have no hen in his head.

DOCTOR

But the lady doctor said it warn't so good — effie-cacious she called it — withouten you took two bottles o' the buildin' up medicine, a box o' the liver pills an' a bottle o' the hair fluid.

GIZ

She knowed a lot. She told me just how I felt an' she said she hated to trouble me but I had a internal ailment. An' she said I needed all their medicine jus' like the Indians used it. But I told her I didn't have no money so she said maybe the box o' liver pills would do if I'd bring 'em some corn for their supper.

DOCTOR

Y' got the liver pills?

GIZ

Uh-huh.

LUT'ER

Took any?

GIZ

Nup, I'm savin' 'em.

LUT'ER

What fur?

GIZ

Till I'm feelin' sicker'n I am now.

DOCTOR

Where are they?

GIZ

In m' pocket.

[*They chew in silence for a minute.*

DOCTOR

Yes, sir! It smelled like ker'sene ter me —

and ker'sene 't wuz. . . . Ker'sene'll cure
heaps o' things if you use it right.
[*He punctuates his talk with covert glances at
Giz. His thoughts are on the pills.*

DOCTOR
Which pocket yer pills in, Giz?

GIZ (*discouragingly*)
M' hip pocket.
[*Again they chew.*

DOCTOR
The Family Medicine Book where I learned ter
be a doctor said camphor an' ker'sene an' lard
rubbed on flannel an' put on the chest 'ud cure
tizic, maybe. (*He looks at Giz*)

DOCTOR
An' what ud cure tizic ought ter cure anything,
I think. . . . I'd 'a' cured m' second wife if the
winder hadn't blowed out an' she got kivered
with snow. After that she jus' wheezed until
she couldn't wheeze no longer. An' so when I
went courtin' m' third wife, I took a stitch in
time an' told her about the camphor an' ker'sen
an' lard. (*Ruefully*) She's a tur'ble healthy
woman. (*His feelings and his curiosity having
overcome his tact, he blurts out*) Giz, why'n
th' hell don't yer show us yer pills!

GIZ
Well — if yer wanner see 'em — here they air.
[*He takes the dirty, mashed box out of his hip
pocket and hands it to the Doctor.*
The Doctor opens the box and smells the pills.

DOCTOR
Ker'sene. . . . Smell 'em Lut'er. (*He holds
the box close to Lut'er's nose*)

LUT'ER (*with the least possible expenditure of energy*)
Uh!

DOCTOR
Ker'sene! . . . Well, I guess it's good for the liver, too. . . . Gimme one, Giz?

GIZ
I ain't got so many I can be givin' 'em ter everybody.

DOCTOR
Jus' one, Giz.

GIZ
She said I ought ter take 'em all fer a cure.

LUT'ER
What yer got, Giz? (*Calling a man by name is a great effort for Lut'er*)

GIZ
Mostly a tired feelin' an' sometimes a crick in th' back. (*Lut'er displays a sympathy undreamed of*)

LUT'ER
Gimme one, Giz.

GIZ
Gosh! You want th' whole box, don't yer?

LUT'ER
Keep yer pills. (*He spits*)

DOCTOR
What's ailin' *you*, Lut'er?

LUT'ER
Oh, a tired feelin' (*there is a long moment of suspended animation, but the Doctor knows that the mills of the gods grind slowly — and he waits for Lut'er to continue*) an' a crick in m' back.

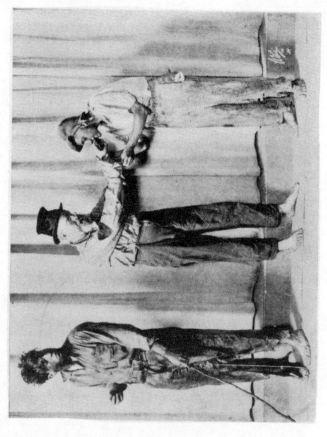

"The Medicine-Show"

The Doctor "swaps" a chew of tobacco for a pill from Giz

DOCTOR

    I'll cure yer, Lut'er. (*Lut'er just looks*) If that Kickapoo doctor with the p'inted muss-tash kin cure yer, I guess I can.

GIZ (*who has been thinking pretty hard*) Got any terbaccer, Doc?

DOCTOR

    Yep.

GIZ

    Well, here's a pill fer a chaw. (*He and the Doctor rise*)

    [*Giz takes a pill out of the box and the Doctor takes his tobacco from his pocket, reaches out his hand for the pill and holds out the tobacco placing his thumb definitely on the plug so that Giz can bite off so much and no more. Giz bites and the Doctor takes over the pill.*

    Lut'er not to be outdone takes a battered plug of tobacco from his pocket and bites off an unlimited " chaw."

    The Doctor takes his knife from his pocket and cuts the pill, smelling it.

DOCTOR

    Ker'sene! (*He tastes it*) Ker'sene! Now I been thinkin' things over, Lut'er and Giz . . .

    [*He tastes the pill again.*

    Ker'sene, sure!

    [*He sits down on the log once more, spits carefully and crosses his legs.*

    I got a business proposition to make.

    [*Silence.*

    Lut'er spits and crosses his legs, and Giz just spits.

DOCTOR

There ain't enough home industry here in Rock Springs. We got a canning fact'ry and a stea'mill; but here comes a medicine show from Ioway — a Kickapoo Indian Medicine Show from Ioway! Now — what we need in Rock Springs is a medicine show! (*He waits for the effect upon his audience*)

LUT'ER (*after a pause*)

How yer goin' ter git it?

DOCTOR

Well, here's my proposition. Ain't we got as much horse sense as them Ioway Indians?

LUT'ER

A damn sight more. (*That is the evident answer to the Doctor, but Lut'er develops a further idea*) We got the country from the Indians.

GIZ (*after a moment of accumulating admiration*)

By golly, Lut'er, yer right.

DOCTOR

Now, I got some medicine science. I'd 'a' cured my second wife if it hadn't been for that busted winder.

GIZ

Yeh, but what come o' yer first wife?

DOCTOR

I could 'a' cured her, too, only I hadn't found the Family Medicine Book then.

LUT'ER

Well, what I wanter know is — what's yer proposition . . . I'm in a hurry. . . . Here comes the *Hattie Brown*.

80

[*The Hattie Brown and the whistle of the stea'mill indicate noon.*
Lut'er takes in the line — removes the fishing worm and puts it in his pocket.

DOCTOR
Well, I'll make the salve an' do the talkin'; Giz'll sort o' whoop things up a bit and Lut'er'll git cured.

LUT'ER
What'll I git cured of?

DOCTOR
Oh, lumbago an' tired feelin' . . . crick in the back and tizic.

LUT'ER
But who'll take a egg out o' somebody's ear?

DOCTOR
Giz'll learn that.

LUT'ER (*with a wan smile that memory illuminates*)
An' who'll play the pianny?

DOCTOR
Besteena, my daughter.

LUT'ER
Where we goin'?

DOCTOR
We'll go ter Lavanny first.

LUT'ER
How'll we git there?

DOCTOR
Walk — unless somebody gives us a tote.

GIZ
We kin go in my John-boat.

LUT'ER

Who'll row?   (*There is fear in his voice*)

GIZ

We'll take turns.   (*Lut'er looks with terror upon Giz*)

LUT'ER

How fur is it?

DOCTOR

Three an' a half mile. . . . Will yer go, Lut'er?

LUT'ER (*evidently thinking deeply*)

How fur is it?

GIZ

Three an' a half mile.

DOCTOR

Will yer go, Lut'er?

LUT'ER

Uh-h.

DOCTOR

Huh?

GIZ

He said, uh-huh.

[*Lut'er chews in silence.*

DOCTOR

I thought he said uh-uh.

GIZ

He said uh-huh.

DOCTOR

He didn't say nothin' o' the sort — he said uh-uh.

[*They turn to Lut'er questioningly. He is chewing intensely.*

LUT'ER (*after a moment*)

How fur did yer say it wuz?

DOCTOR

Three an' a half mile.

[*Silence.*

GIZ

We'll each take a oar.

[*Silence.*
A stentorian voice is heard calling Stee'vun.
The Doctor rises, hastily.

DOCTOR

What d'yer say, Lut'er?

LUT'ER

It's three an' a half mile ter Lavanny — an' three an' a half mile back. . . . Pretty fur.

DOCTOR

We kin come back on the current.

LUT'ER

Three an' a half mile air three an' a half mile — current or no current.

[*Again the masterful female voice calls Stee'-*
vun. There is no mistaking its meaning.
The Doctor is torn between home and business.
Lut'er takes up his rod, rebaits the hook with
the fishing-worm from his pocket and casts his
line into the river.

LUT'ER

I'll think it over . . . but I ain't givin' yuh no hope . . . Three an' a half mile one way air pretty fur . . . but two ways — it's turruble!

DOCTOR

Come on, Giz. We'll talk it over.

[*The Doctor and Giz leave Lut'er to his prob-*
lem.
Lut'er is undecided. He is at a crisis in his life.

83

He spits thoughtfully and looks after the re-treating Doctor and Giz.

LUT'ER

Three an' a half mile . . . (*He takes in his line and removes the fishing-worm. He rises and looks again after the Doctor and Giz. He hesitates*) . . . two ways . . . (*He starts in the opposite direction, as he justifies himself to his inner self*) Rock Springs is fur enough fur me! (*When he disappears the play is over.*)

SIX WHO PASS WHILE THE LENTILS
BOIL

THE BOY
THE QUEEN
THE MIME
THE MILKMAID
THE BLINDMAN
THE BALLAD-SINGER
THE DREADFUL HEADSMAN
YOU (*in the audience*)

The Scene is a kitchen.
The Period is when you will.

[Before the opening of the curtains the Prologue enters upon the forestage and summons the Device-Bearer who carries a large copper pot.

PROLOGUE

This is a copper pot. (*The Device-Bearer shows it to the audience carefully*) It is filled with boiling water. (*The Device-Bearer makes the sound of bubbling water*) It is on the fire. See the flames. (*The Device-Bearer sets the pot in the center of the forestage and blows under it with a pair of bellows*) And see the water boiling over. (*The Device-Bearer again makes the sound of bubbling water and then withdraws to where he can see the play from the side of the forestage*) We are looking into the kitchen of the Boy whose mother left him alone. I do not know where she has gone but I do know that he is gathering lentils now.

YOU

What are lentils?

PROLOGUE

A lentil? Why a lentil, don't you see, is not a bean nor yet a pea; but it is kin to both . . . You must imagine that the boy has built the fire and set the water boiling. He is very industrious but you need not feel sorry for him. His mother is very good to him and he is safe. Are

87

you ready now? . . . Very well. Be quiet.
[*The Prologue claps his hands twice.*

The curtains open and a kitchen is disclosed.
There are a bench, a stool and a cupboard. A
great door at the back opens into a corridor.
There are also two windows — one higher than
the other looking upon the corridor. At the
right a door opens into the bedroom of the Boy's
mother. A great pewter spoon lies upon the
shelf in the cupboard.
A large Butterfly comes in through the door-
way, flits about and looks off stage.
The song of the Boy is heard from the garden.
The Butterfly goes to the door, poises a moment,
then alights on the cupboard.
The Boy enters with a great bowl filled with
lentils.
The Butterfly flies to the bowl and satisfied
returns to the cupboard.
The Boy smiles at the Butterfly but he does
not touch him. Then he empties the lentils into
the pot and water splashes on his careless hand.
A moan is heard in the distance. The Boy and
the Butterfly go to the door.
The Queen's voice is heard calling:
Butterfly, Butterfly, where shall I hide?
[*Enter the Queen.*

QUEEN

Boy, Boy — oh, I am distraught!

YOU

What is distraught?

PROLOGUE

Distraught means distracted, perplexed, beset
with doubt, worried by some fear.

BOY (*pityingly*)
Why are you distraught?

QUEEN
Oh — Oh — Oh — They are going to behead me!

BOY
When?

QUEEN
Before mid-day.

BOY
Why are they going to behead you? Is it a story? Tell it to me.

QUEEN
I was guilty of a breach of etiquette.

BOY
What is that?

QUEEN
I did something that was considered bad manners and the law says the punishment is decapitation.

YOU
What is decapitation?

PROLOGUE
Decapitation is beheading; cutting off one's head.

BOY
Why, only kings and queens can be decapitated.

QUEEN
Oh, I know — I know —

BOY (*disappointed*)
Are you a queen?

QUEEN
Yes.

BOY

I thought all queens were big. My mother says they are always regal. And my mother knows.

QUEEN

Oh, I *am* the queen. *I am* the queen; but I am so unhappy.

BOY

My mother told me kings and queens knew no fear? Why, you're afraid.

QUEEN

Oh, Boy, Boy, I *am* your queen and I *am* afraid and unhappy. And queens are just like other people when they are afraid and unhappy.

BOY (*disappointed*)

Aren't they always regal?

QUEEN

No — no. Oh, little boy, hide me, hide me from the Dreadful Headsman!

BOY

I haven't any place to hide you. You couldn't get under the bench and you couldn't get into the cupboard.

QUEEN

Little boy, can't you see that I shall lose my head if I am found?

BOY

You might have hidden in the pot if I hadn't put it on the fire.

QUEEN

Oh — Oh — Oh —

BOY

I'm sorry.

QUEEN

I am distraught.

BOY

Well, I'll hide you, because you are distraught;
but — I am not sure you are a queen . . .
Where's your crown?   You can't be a queen
without a crown!

[*She reaches up to her head.*

QUEEN

Oh, I was running so fast that it must have
slipped from my head.   (*Sees the Butterfly*)
Butterfly, tell him I am your Queen.

[*The Butterfly flies to her head and lights on
her disheveled locks like a diadem.*

BOY

Oh, I have talked to the Queen! . . . You can
hide in my mother's bed-room in there; but first
please tell me a story.

QUEEN

They will find me here.   I'll tell you a story
afterward.

BOY

I want you to tell me now.

QUEEN

Well, you watch at the door and warn me when
you see someone coming.   (*The Butterfly
brushes her ear*)   But stay, the Butterfly says
he'll watch.

[*The Butterfly goes to the door.*

BOY

Will he know?

QUEEN

Oh, yes.   He is a wonderful butterfly — wise
beyond his years.

BOY

Sit down and tell me your story.   (*He places*

a black pillow for the Queen on the step and an orange pillow for himself)

QUEEN

Last night we celebrated the second year of peace with the neighboring kingdom. We were dancing the minuet just after the banquet, when I stepped on the ring-toe of my husband the King's great aunt.

BOY

Didn't you say excuse me?

QUEEN

It was useless. The law says that if a queen steps on the ring-toe of the King's great aunt or any member of her family the Queen must be beheaded while the King's four clocks are striking twelve at mid-day.

BOY

Oh, that means to-day?

QUEEN

Yes.

BOY

Why, it's almost mid-day now. See, I've just set the lentils boiling.

QUEEN

If you can hide me until after the King's four clocks strike twelve I shall be safe.

BOY

Why are there four clocks?

QUEEN

Because the law allows only one clock for each tower in the castle.

BOY

Then I hear all the King's clocks every day!

There's a big clock, and two clocks not so big,
and a tiny little clock.

QUEEN

Yes, those are the four.

BOY

Why will you be safe *after* the four clocks strike
twelve?

QUEEN

Because that is the law.

BOY

Aren't laws funny?

QUEEN

Funny?   This one is very sad, I think.

BOY

Mightn't it be twelve any mid-day?

QUEEN

No; the Prime Minister of my grandfather who
passed the law decided that it meant only the
following mid-day.

BOY (*rising and rushing to the door*)

They'll find you here.

QUEEN (*rising calmly*)

Oh, no, this is the short cut to the beheading
block.   Through that corridor.

BOY

Why didn't you run the other way?

QUEEN

Because they always search for escaped people
in that direction.   So I ran through your garden and into this room.   They'll never search
for me so close to the castle.

BOY

How did you escape?

93

QUEEN

  I —

  [*The Butterfly seems agitated.*

BOY

  You —

QUEEN

  Someone is coming. Hide me!

BOY

  In here — in my mother's room. 'Sh! 'Sh!

  [*The Queen goes out.*

  Enter the Mime.

  He pokes his head in the lower window and

  peeps around the door.

  The boy turns.

BOY (*weakly*)

  Are you the Dreadful Headsman?

MIME

  What?

BOY

  Are you the Dreadful Headsman?

MIME

  Do I look like a headsman?

BOY

  I don't know; I've never seen one.

MIME

  Well, suppose I am.

BOY

  Are you?

MIME

  Maybe I am.

BOY

  Oh!

MIME

  Booh!

BOY
  I'm — I'm — not afraid.
MIME
  Bah!
BOY
  And my mother isn't here.
MIME
  Br — r — r — r!
  [*The Boy reaches for his knife.*
MIME
  Bing!
BOY
  I wasn't going to hurt you!
MIME
  'Sh! . . . 'Sh! . . . 'Sh! . . .
BOY
  I'll give you my knife if you'll go 'way.
MIME
  Ah,— ha!
BOY
  It's nearly mid-day and you'd better **go.**
MIME
  Well, give me the knife.
BOY
  Promise me to go.
MIME (*laughs, turning away*)
  Aren't you going to the beheading?
BOY
  No.   I have to boil the lentils for our mid-day
  meal.
MIME
  May I come back and eat some?
BOY
  You'll have to ask my mother.

MIME

Where is she?

BOY

She's over that way.   She went to the market to buy a bobbin.

YOU

What is a bobbin?

PROLOGUE

A bobbin is a spool upon which thread is wound, and it is sharp at one end so that it can be easily passed backward and forward, to and fro, through the other threads in making lace.

MIME (*starting off*)

Well, I'll be back to eat some lentils.

BOY (*too eagerly*)

You'd better hurry.

MIME

You seem to want to get rid of me.

BOY (*allaying suspicion*)

Well, I think you'd better go or you'll be late — and it's very wrong to be late.

MIME (*going toward the door*)

I think I'll (*changing his mind*) sit down.

BOY (*disappointed*)

Oh!

MIME

What would you say if I wasn't the Headsman?

BOY

But you said you were.

MIME

I said *maybe* I was.

BOY

Aren't you?

MIME
Maybe I'm not.

BOY
Honest?

MIME
Um, hum.

BOY (*relieved*)
Oh! . . .

MIME
You *were* afraid.

BOY
No . . . I wasn't.

MIME
Would you fight?

BOY
You bet I would.

MIME
It wouldn't take me a minute to lick you.

BOY
Maybe it wouldn't, but I wouldn't give up right away. That would be cowardly. . . . Who are you?

MIME
I'm a mime —

BOY
What's a mime?

MIME
A mime's a mime.

BOY
Go on and tell me.

MIME
A mime's a mountebank.

BOY
What's a mountebank?

MIME

A mountebank's a strolling player.

BOY

Are you going to perform for me?

MIME

Not to-day — I'm on my way to the decapitation.

BOY

Do you want to see the decapitation?

MIME

Well, yes. But most of all I want to pick up
a few coins.

BOY

How?

MIME

Why, I'll perform after the Queen has lost her
head.

BOY

Won't you be too sorry?

MIME

No. You see, I'll be thinking mostly about
what I'm going to do. I have to do my best
because it is hard to be more interesting than a
decapitation. And after it's all over the crowd
will begin to talk and to move about: and I'll
have to rush up to the front of them and cry
out at the top of my lungs, "Stop — Ho, for
Jack the Juggler! Would you miss him? In
London where the king of kings lives, all the
knights and ladies of the Court would leave a
crowning to watch Jack the Juggler toss three
golden balls with one hand or balance a weathervane upon his nose." Then a silence will come
upon the crowd and they will all turn to me.

Someone will say, "Where is this Jack the Juggler?" And I shall answer, "Jack the Juggler, the greatest of the great, the pet of kings, entertainer to the Pope and the joy of Cathay stands before you." And I'll throw back my cloak and stand revealed. So! Someone will then shout, "Let us have it, Jack." So I'll draw my three golden balls from my pouch — like this — and then begin.

[*The Boy is watching breathlessly and the Butterfly is interested too. Their disappointment is keen when Jack does nothing.*

BOY

Aren't you going to show me?

MIME

No, I must be off.

BOY

Aren't you ever coming back?

MIME

Maybe, yes; perhaps, no.

BOY

I'll give you some lentils if you'll juggle the balls for me.

MIME (*sniffs the pot*)

They aren't cooked yet.

BOY

Let me hold your golden balls.

MIME (*Takes a gold ball from his pouch and lets the Boy hold it*)

Here's one.

BOY

And do they pay you well?

MIME (*taking the ball from the Boy*)

Ay, that they do. If I am as interesting as the

beheading I'll get perhaps fifteen farthings in money and other things that I can exchange for food and raiment.

BOY

I'm going to be a mime and buy a castle and a sword.

MIME

Maybe so and maybe not. Who knows? . . . Good-bye. (*He goes out*)

BOY (*to the Butterfly*)

If he had been the Dreadful Headsman I would have slain him. So! . . . " Ah, wicked headsman, you shall not behead the Queen! . . . Cross not that threshold or I'll run you through."

[*Throughout this the Butterfly shows great interest and enters into the spirit of it, being absorbed at times and frightened at others. Enter the Milkmaid at door.*

MILKMAID

Pst! . . . Pst!

BOY (*startled*)

Oh!

MILKMAID

Are you going to the decapitation?

BOY

No. Are you?

MILKMAID

That I am.

BOY

Will your mother let you go?

MILKMAID

She doesn't know.

BOY

Did you run away?

MILKMAID

No.   I went out to milk the cow.

BOY

And did you do it?

MILKMAID

Yes.

BOY

Why didn't you wait until you came back?

MILKMAID

My mother was looking and I had to let her see me doing something.

BOY

How did you get away when you took the milk pails into the house?

MILKMAID

I didn't take them in.   As soon as my mother turned her back I hid the pails and I ran through here to take a short cut.

BOY

Where did you hide the milk?

MILKMAID

In the hollow tree.

BOY

Won't it sour?

MILKMAID

Maybe.

BOY

Won't your mother scold you?

MILKMAID

Yes, of course, but I couldn't miss the beheading.

BOY

Will you take the sour milk home?

MILKMAID

Yes, and after my mother scolds me I'll make it into nice cheese and sell it to the King's Cook and then mother will forgive me.

BOY (*sniffing the pot*)

You'd better hurry. It's nearly mid-day. Don't you smell the lentils?

MILKMAID

The headsman hasn't started yet.

BOY (*giggling*)

He'd better hurry.

MILKMAID

They can't find the Queen.

BOY (*so innocently*)

Did she escape?

MILKMAID

Yes.

BOY

Are they hunting for her?

MILKMAID

Yes, and they've offered a big reward to the person who finds her.

BOY

How much?

MILKMAID

A pail of gold and a pair of finger rings.

BOY

That's a good deal . . . with a pail of gold I could buy my mother a velvet dress and a silken kerchief and a bonnet made of cloth of gold — and I could buy myself a milk-white palfry.

MILKMAID

And you'd never have to work again.

BOY

But she's such a gentle queen. Where are they hunting her?

MILKMAID

Everywhere.

BOY

Everywhere! . . . Maybe she's waiting at the beheading block.

MILKMAID

Silly goose! She wouldn't try to escape this way. She'd go in the opposite direction.

BOY

Do people always run in the opposite direction?

MILKMAID

Of course, everybody knows that.

BOY

I wish I could go.

MILKMAID

Come on.

BOY

Um — uh. The lentils might burn.

MILKMAID

Pour some cold water on them.

BOY

Um — uh. I promised I wouldn't leave the house.

MILKMAID

Oh, it will be wonderful!

BOY

The Mime will be there.

MILKMAID

The one with the long cloak and the golden balls?

BOY

Um — uh.

MILKMAID

Ooh!

BOY

How did you know?

MILKMAID

I saw him on the way to the market one day —
and when my mother wasn't looking at me I
gave him a farthing.

BOY

Is he a good juggler?

MILKMAID

He's magic! Why, he can throw three golden
balls in the air and catch them with one hand
and then keep them floating in the air in a circle.

BOY

And can he balance a weathervane on his nose
while it's turning?

MILKMAID

Yes, and he can balance an egg on the end of a
long stick that is balanced on his chin!

BOY

Oh — I wish I could see him. (*Looks at the
pot to see if the lentils are done*)

MILKMAID

Come on!

BOY

Well — (*Begins to weaken and just as he is
about to start, the Butterfly flits past him into
the Queen's room*)

MILKMAID

Oh — what a lovely butterfly!

BOY

No — No — I can't go.   But you had better hurry.

MILKMAID

Well, I'll try to catch the butterfly first.

BOY

Oh, no, you mustn't touch that butterfly.

MILKMAID

Why?

BOY

Because — because he's my friend.

MILKMAID

Silly!

BOY

He *is* a good friend and he's the wisest butterfly in the world.

MILKMAID

What can he do?

BOY

He can almost talk.

MILKMAID

Almost? . . . Oh, I know.   I'm a goose.   You want to play a trick on me so I'll miss the beheading.

BOY

You'd better hurry.

MILKMAID

I wish you'd come.

BOY (*sadly*)

I can't.   I've a duty to perform.

MILKMAID

Aren't duties always hard?   (*Both sigh*)
[*She takes up her milk pail.*

BOY

What are you going to do with that pail?

MILKMAID

I'm going to stand on it. . . . Good-bye. (*She goes out*)

BOY

Good-bye. (*He watches for a moment, then goes to the pot and tries the lentils; then whispers through door to the Queen*) The lentils are getting soft.

[*There is a fumbling in the passage and a voice is heard,* Help the blind. Help the blind. *The Butterfly returns to the top of the cupboard. The Blindman appears at the door.*

PROLOGUE

He's blind, but he'll show you how the blind can see.

BLINDMAN (*sniffing*)

Cooking lentils?

BOY

Yes.

BLINDMAN

Cook, which way to the beheading?

BOY

Keep straight ahead — the way you are going, old man.

BLINDMAN

Don't you want to take me with you?

BOY

I'm not going.

BLINDMAN

Not going to the beheading?

BOY

No, I have to cook the lentils.

BLINDMAN
   Come on and go with me and maybe I'll give
   you a farthing.
BOY
   I can't.
BLINDMAN
   Yes, you can.   Who else is here?
BOY (*swallowing: it's hard to fib*)
   No one.
BLINDMAN
   Can't you run away?   Your mother won't know
   you've gone.
BOY
   It's my duty to stay here.
BLINDMAN
   It's your duty to help a poor, blindman, little
   boy.
BOY
   Are you stone blind?
BLINDMAN
   Yes.
BOY
   Then how did you know I was a *little* boy?
BLINDMAN
   Because you *sound* like a little boy.
BOY
   Well, if you're stone blind why do you want to
   go to the beheading?
BLINDMAN
   I can see with my ears.
BOY
   Aw —
BLINDMAN
   Didn't I know you were a little boy?

BOY
Yes, but you had to guess twice. First you
thought I was a cook.

BLINDMAN
Well, aren't you cooking lentils?

BOY
Yes; but you can smell them.

BLINDMAN
Well, I see with my nose, too.

BOY
Aw — how can you see with your nose?

BLINDMAN
If you give me some bread I'll show you.

BOY
I can't give you any bread, but I'll give you some
raw lentils.

BLINDMAN
All right. Give me lentils.

BOY
. . . I'll put them by the pot — Ready.

BLINDMAN
All right. (*Sniffs. Walks to the pot and gets
lentils and puts them in an old pouch*) Isn't
that seeing with my nose?

BOY
H'm! (*in wonder*) Now see with your ears
and I'll give you some more lentils.

BLINDMAN
All right. Speak.
[*The Boy gets behind the stool and speaks.
The Blindman goes toward him. The Boy
moves around stealthily.*

BLINDMAN
You're cheating. You've moved.

BOY (*jumping up on the bench*)
  Well, where am I?

BLINDMAN
  You're standing on something.

BOY
  How did you guess it?

BLINDMAN
  I didn't guess it. I know it.

BOY
  Why can't I do that?

BLINDMAN
  You can if you try; but it takes practice.

BOY
  Can you see the door now?

BLINDMAN
  No. I've turned around too many times. Besides there is more than one door.

BOY
  Oh — m-m . . . You aren't really blind!

BLINDMAN
  Blind people learn to use what they have. Once I too could see with my eyes.

BOY
  Just like me?

BLINDMAN
  Yes. And then I didn't take the trouble to see with my ears and my nose and my fingers — after I became blind I had to learn . . . Why, I can tell whether a man who passes me at the palace gate is a poor man or a noble or a merchant.

BOY
  How can you do that?

BLINDMAN

By the sound of the step.

BOY

Aw — how can you do that?

BLINDMAN

Shut your eyes and try it.

BOY

Well, I know what you are. That would be easy.

BLINDMAN

I'll pretend I'm somebody else. (*Feels with his stick; touches bench. Feels around again*)

BOY

Why are you doing that?

BLINDMAN

To see how far I can walk without bumping into something.

BOY

Um —

BLINDMAN

Ready.

BOY (*hides face in hands*)

Yes.

BLINDMAN

Don't peep. (*The Boy tries hard not to*)

BOY

I won't.

BLINDMAN

All ready (*shuffles like a commoner*). Who was it?

BOY

A poor man.

BLINDMAN

See how easy?

BOY

I could see him as plain as if I had my eyes open . . . Now try me again.

BLINDMAN

Ready.

BOY

All right.   (*The Blindman seems to grow in height.   His face is filled with a rare brightness. He steadies himself a moment and then walks magnificently down the room*)

BOY (*in beautiful wonder*)

A noble!   I could see him.

BLINDMAN

All you have to do is try.

BOY

I always thought it was terrible to be blind.

BLINDMAN

Sometimes it is.

BOY

But I thought everything was black.

BLINDMAN

It used to be until I taught myself how to see.

BOY

Why is it terrible sometimes?

BLINDMAN

Because I cannot help the poor who need help. If I had money I could feed the hungry and clothe the poor little beggar children in winter!

BOY

Would a pail of gold and a pair of finger rings help you feed the hungry and clothe the poor, little beggar children in winter?

BLINDMAN

A pail of gold! I have dreamed of what I might do with so much wealth!

BOY

I can get a pail of gold if I break a promise.

BLINDMAN

Would *you* break a promise?

BOY

. . . No — but — No!

BLINDMAN

Of course you wouldn't.

BOY

I couldn't break a promise for *two* pails of gold.

BLINDMAN

Nor twenty-two, little boy.

BOY

When you walked like a noble I saw a beautiful man behind my eyes with a crown of gold.

BLINDMAN

If you broke a promise for a pail of gold and two finger rings you would never see a beautiful noble with a crown of gold when you closed your eyes . . .

BOY

Can blind men see beautiful things even when it's rainy?

BLINDMAN

Blindmen can always see beautiful things if they try. Clouds and rain are beautiful to me — and when I get wet I think of the sunshine. I saw sunshine with my eyes when I was a little boy. Now I see it with my whole body when it warms me. I saw rain with my eyes when I was a little boy. Now I see it with my hands when it falls

on them — drop — drop — drop — dropity —
dropity — and I love it because it makes the
lentils grow.

BOY

I never thought of that.   Rain makes me stay
indoors and I never like it except in June.

BLINDMAN

You don't have to stay in for long.

BOY

Can blind men see beautiful things in a beheading?

BLINDMAN

No.   But I must be there with the crowd.   I
shall tell stories to the people and perhaps they
will give me food or money.

BOY

Can't you stay and tell me stories?

BLINDMAN

No.   I must be on my way . . . If I do not see
the beheading I cannot tell about it when I meet
someone who was not there.   Oh, I shall make
a thrilling tale of it.

BOY

Tell it to me when you come back. .

BLINDMAN

If you give me some cooked lentils.

BOY

I'll save you some.

BLINDMAN

Are the lentils nearly done?

BOY

Half.

BLINDMAN

I must be on my way then . . . Good-bye.

(*Starting to go in the wrong direction*)

BOY

  Here's the door.

BLINDMAN

  Thank you, little boy . . . Don't forget to see
  with your ears and nose and fingers.
  [*The Blindman goes out.*

BOY

  I won't.

BLINDMAN

  Good-bye.

BOY

  Good-bye.   (*The Boy covers his eyes and tries
  to see with his ears and his nose*)   It's easier
  with the ears.
  [*Singing is heard.*
  Enter the Ballad-Singer.
  Hello!

BOY

  Hello!

SINGER

  How are you?

BOY

  I'm very well.

SINGER

  That's good.

BOY

  Thank you.

SINGER

  Cooking?

BOY

  Yes.

SINGER (*coming into the room*)

  Something good?

BOY
  Lentils.
SINGER
  Give me some?
BOY
  They aren't done.
SINGER
  Nearly.   I can smell them.
BOY
  Do you like them?
SINGER
  When I'm hungry.
BOY
  Are you hungry now?
SINGER
  I'm always hungry.   (*They laugh*)
BOY
  Were you singing?
SINGER
  Yes.
BOY
  Do you like to sing?
SINGER
  When I get something for my ballads.
BOY
  Are you a ballad-singer?
SINGER
  Yes.
BOY
  Sing one for me?
SINGER
  Give me some lentils?
BOY
  I'll give you some raw lentils.

SINGER

I want some of the cooked ones.

BOY

They aren't done.

SINGER

Are they nearly done?

BOY

More than half.

SINGER

I like them that way.

BOY

All right.　Sing me a ballad.

SINGER

Well, give me the lentils first.

BOY

Oh, no, sing the ballad first.

SINGER

No, sir, give me the lentils first.

BOY

That isn't fair.

SINGER

Why not?　After I sing to you maybe you won't pay me.

BOY

Yes, I will.

SINGER

Then why not pay me first?

BOY

You might not sing.

SINGER (*laughing*)

Yes, I will.

BOY (*laughing*)

Well, I'll give you some lentils at the end of each verse.

SINGER
> That's a bargain.

BOY
> Sing.

SINGER (*sings one line*)
> Six stalwart sons the miller had —
> Give me the lentils.

BOY
> Finish that verse.

SINGER
> I did finish it.

BOY
> Now that's not fair.   You only sang a line.

SINGER
> Well, a line's a verse.

BOY (*with a gesture that indicates how long a verse ought to be*)
> I meant a whole verse.

SINGER (*mimicking the gesture*)
> A line's a whole verse.

BOY
> Oh, now, be fair, I mean a *whole,* whole verse.

SINGER
> You mean a *stanza.*

BOY
> I always heard it called a verse.

SINGER
> Well, keep the bargain.   I sang a verse.   Give me some lentils.

BOY (*rising and taking a very few lentils on his spoon*)
> Next time I mean a stanza . . . Here are some lentils.

[*The Ballad-Singer eyes the meager portion, cools it and eats.*

SINGER
 Stingy.

BOY
 Isn't that *some* lentils?

SINGER (*laughs*)
 Well —

BOY
 Now begin again.

SINGER
 At the end of every stanza a spoonful of lentils.

BOY
 I didn't say a spoonful.

SINGER (*starts to go*)
 Very well, I won't sing a ballad.

BOY
 All right. I'll give you a spoonful at the end of each — stanza. (*He sits on the floor by the pot of lentils*)

SINGER (*sings*)

The Ballad of the Miller and His Six Sons

Six stalwart sons the miller had
All brave and fair to see —
He taught them each a worthy trade —
And they grew gallantly.
Tara — da — da — da-da-da — da-da-da
Tara — da — da — da-de — da-dee.
Give me some lentils.

BOY
 Here . . . Hurry up.

SINGER (*sings*)
 The first was John of the dimpled chin

"Six who pass while the Lentils Boil"
The Boy and the Ballad Singer

And a fist of iron had he —
He learned to wield the broadsword well
And turned to soldiery.
Tara — da — da, etc.

BOY
Please! Please don't stop.

SINGER
Keep to the bargain.

BOY
Here, take two spoonfuls and finish without
stopping.

SINGER (*sings rest of ballad*)
The second son was christened Hugh
And curly locks had he —
He learned to use the tabor and lute
And turned to minstrelsy.
Tara — da — da, etc.

The third was James of the gentle ways
And speech of gold had he —
He learned his psalms and learned his creed
And turned to simony.
Tara — da — da, etc.

The fourth was Dick of the hazel eye,
And a steady hand had he —
With a hammer and saw and a chest of tools
He turned to carpentry.
Tara — da — da, etc.

The fifth was Ned of the velvet tread
And feather fingers had he.
He used his gifts in a naughty way
And turned to burglary.
Tara — da — da, etc.

The sixth was Robin, surnamed the Rare,
For always young was he —
He learned the joy of this sunny world
And turned to poetry.
Tara — da — da, etc.

The Miller approached three score and ten
A happy man was he
His five good sons and the one who was bad,
All turned to gallantry.
Tara — da — da, etc.

BOY

Sing me another.

SINGER

A spoonful at the end of every stanza.

BOY

Don't stop after you begin.

SINGER

Pay me in advance.

BOY

I suppose I'll have to.   (*He feeds the Ballad-Singer*)

SINGER (*sings second ballad*)

The Ballad of the Three Little Pigs

Two little pigs were pink — pink — pink —
And one little pig was black — black —
The three little pigs were very good friends,
But one little pig was black — black.

Three little pigs would play — play — play —
But one little pig was black — black —
And three little pigs would have a jolly time
Though one little pig was black — black.

Three little pigs soon grew — grew — grew —
And one little pig was black — black.
The three little pigs became fat hogs —
And one fat hog was black — black.

The two fat hogs were pink — pink — pink —
And one fat hog was black — black.
The three fat hogs all made good ham,
Though one fat hog was black — black.

BOY
Sing me another.

SINGER
I can't.   I'm tired.

BOY
Are you going to sing those at the beheading?

SINGER
What beheading?

BOY
At the Queen's beheading.

SINGER
Where?

BOY
Over there.

SINGER
When?

BOY
To-day.

SINGER
I must be going.   Certainly I'll sing there and
I'll take up a collection.

BOY
It's going to be before the King's four clocks
strike twelve.

SINGER
>It's nearly time now. If I can collect a piece of gold I can buy a vermillion robe and sing at the King's court.

BOY
>I could collect a pail of gold and two finger rings and sit at the feet of the King if I'd break a promise.

SINGER
>Perhaps you will.

BOY
>Would you?

SINGER
>I'd rather sing along the highway all my life. It is better to dream of a vermillion robe than to have one that is not honestly got.

BOY
>The Blindman said something like that.

SINGER
>Who said what?

BOY
>The Blindman said if I broke a promise I'd never again see a beautiful noble with a golden crown when I closed my eyes.

SINGER
>He was right.

BOY
>When you get your vermillion robe will you let me see it?

SINGER
>That I will . . . Good-bye.

BOY
>Good-bye. (*Singer goes out*)

BOY (*hums a snatch of the ballads*)
[*The Headsman steps into the door and plants
his axe beside him for an impressive picture.
The Boy turns and starts in terror.*

HEADSMAN
Have you seen the Queen?

BOY
Sir?

HEADSMAN
Have you seen the Queen?

BOY
How should I, sir? I've been cooking the lentils.

HEADSMAN
She is here!

BOY
How — could — she — be — here, sir?

HEADSMAN
Well, if she isn't here, where is she?

BOY (*relieved*)
I don't know where she is if she isn't here, sir.

HEADSMAN
She has too much sense to hide so near the
castle and on the short cut to the headsman's
block . . . Do you know who I am?

BOY
I think so — sir.

HEADSMAN
Think? Don't you *know?*

BOY
Yes, sir.

HEADSMAN
Who am I then?

BOY

You're the Dreadful Headsman.

HEADSMAN

I am the winder of the king's four clocks *and* when I am needed I am the best headsman in three kingdoms.   And *this* is my axe.

BOY

Is it sharp?

HEADSMAN

It will split a hare in two.   (*Runs finger near blade meaningly*)

BOY

Oh!

HEADSMAN

A hare in two!

BOY

Would you really cut off the Queen's head?

HEADSMAN

That's my business: to cut off heads and the nobler the head the better my business.

BOY

She's such a nice queen.

HEADSMAN

Have you seen her?

BOY

Y — es, sir.

HEADSMAN

When?

BOY

One day — when I was boiling some lentils.

HEADSMAN

Did you see her neck?

BOY

Yes, sir.

HEADSMAN
  Not much bigger than a hair.
BOY (*desperately friendly*)
  Have you seen my knife?
HEADSMAN (*sharply*)
  I'm talking about the Queen and I'm going to
  talk about myself until I hear the King's trum-
  peter calling me to the beheading.
BOY
  Yes, sir. (*Edging between the bench and door
  of the room where the Queen is hidden*)
HEADSMAN
  Sit down.
BOY
  I' rather stand, sir.
HEADSMAN
  Sit down!   And I'll tell you how I'm going to
  behead the Queen.
BOY
  You can't behead her after the King's four
  clocks have struck twelve.
HEADSMAN
  How did you know that?
BOY (*realizing his blunder*)
  Well —
HEADSMAN
  Nobody knows that except the royal family and
  people of the court.
BOY
  A little — bird told — me.
HEADSMAN
  Where is the little bird that I may cut its head
  off?

BOY

Don't hurt the little bird, but tell me how you are going to behead the Queen.

HEADSMAN

Well — (*At the stool*) This is the block. There's the Queen behind the iron gate. We'll say that door is the gate.

[*The Boy starts.*

And out there is the crowd. Now, I appear like this and walk up the steps. The crowd cheers, so I bow and show myself and my axe. Then I walk over to the gate —

BOY

Don't go in there. That's my mother's room and you might frighten *her.*

HEADSMAN

Who's in your mother's room?

BOY

She is.

HEADSMAN

Well, if she's in there, maybe she'd like to hear my story.

BOY

She's in bed.

HEADSMAN

Sick? (*The Boy nods vigorously*) All right . . . Well, I've bowed to the crowd and I start for the Queen.— If you won't open the door, you pretend you're the Queen.

BOY

I don't want to be the Queen.

HEADSMAN

Come on and pretend. I walk up to the gate — so, and open it and then I say " Your Majesty,

I'm going to cut off your head " and she bows
— *bow* — (*The Boy bows*) And then I say
" Are you ready? " and she says, " I am ready."
Then I blindfold her —

BOY

Now, don't blindfold me, sir!

HEADSMAN

I'm showing you how it's done.

BOY

But if you blindfold me I can't see when you
do it.

HEADSMAN (*admitting the point*)

All right . . . Then I blindfold her and I lead
her to the block and I say, " Have you made
your peace with Heaven? " and she says,
" Yes." . . .

BOY

If you won't tell me any more I'll give you my
knife.

HEADSMAN

Aren't you interested?

BOY

Yes, but your axe is so sharp and it might slip.

HEADSMAN

Sharp? It will cut a hair in two, but I know
how to handle it . . . Come on . . . (*The
Boy reluctantly falls into the picture again*)
And then . . .(*Raising his axe*) And then
. . . (*Headsman sees the Butterfly*) And
then . . . How-d'-ye-do? Butterfly.
[*The Boy runs to the pot unnoticed by the
Headsman.*

BOY

Lentils, lentils, boil the time away

That my good queen may live to-day.
[*The Headsman and the Butterfly are having quite a game.*
Suddenly the great clock begins to strike and the two next larger follow slowly.
The Headsman rushes to the back door with his axe.

HEADSMAN

Why doesn't the trumpeter blow his call!
[*The Boy counts the strokes of the clock and as the third clock strikes twelve he rushes to the door of the bedroom.*

BOY

Queen! Queen! It's mid-day.

HEADSMAN

Queen — Queen — (*He strides to the bedroom and drags the Queen out*) The little clock hasn't struck yet! (*He pulls the Queen toward the rear door and shouts*) Here! Here! don't let the little clock strike! I've won the pail of gold!
[*The Boy has set the bench in the doorway so that the Headsman stumbles. The Butterfly keeps flying against the Headsman's nose, which makes him sneeze.*

BOY

No one heard you!

QUEEN

Let me go! Let me go!

HEADSMAN (*sneezing as only a headsman can*)

The Queen! The Queen!
[*The little clock begins to strike.*
The Boy counts eagerly, one, two, three, etc.

"The Six Who Pass While the Lentils Boil"

The Queen, the defeated Headman, and the Boy

Between strokes the Headsman sneezes and shouts.

The Queen! The Queen!

[*At the fifth stroke the Headsman falls on his knees. The Queen becomes regal, her foot on his neck.*

The Boy kneels at her side.

QUEEN

Base villain! According to the law I am saved! But you are doomed. As Winder of the King's four clocks the law commands that you be decapitated because the four clocks did not strike together. Do you know that law?

HEADSMAN

Oh, Lady, I do, but I did but do my duty. I was sharpening my axe this morning and I couldn't wind the clocks. Intercede for me.

QUEEN

It is useless.

BOY

Is there any other headsman?

QUEEN

The law says the Chief Headsman must behead the chief winder of the King's four clocks.

BOY

Can the Dreadful Headsman behead himself?

QUEEN

Aye, there's the difficulty.

HEADSMAN

Oh, your Majesty, pardon me!

BOY

Yes, pardon him.

QUEEN

On one condition: He is to give his axe to the
museum and devote all his old age to the care
of the King's four clocks. . . . For myself, I
shall pass a law requiring the ladies of the court
to wear no jewels. So, if the King's aunt can
wear no rings, she assuredly cannot have a
ring-toe, and hereafter I may step where I
please. . . . Sir Headsman, lead the way. . . .
And now, my little boy, to you I grant every
Friday afternoon an hour's sport with the
Mime, a spotted cow for the little Milkmaid, a
cushion and a canopy at the palace gate for the
Blindman, a vermillion cloak for the Ballad-
Singer, a velvet gown, a silken kerchief and a
cloth-of-gold bonnet for your mother, and for
yourself a milk-white palfry, two pails of gold,
two finger rings, a castle and a sword. . . .
Arise, Sir Little Boy. . . . Your arm.

BOY

May I take my knife, your Majesty?

QUEEN

That you may. (*He gets the knife and returns
to her. She lays her hand on his arm*) Sir
Headsman, announce our coming.

HEADSMAN

Make way — make way — for her Majesty
the Queen.

QUEEN (*correcting*)

And Sir Little Boy.

HEADSMAN

What's his other name, your Majesty?

BOY (*whispering with the wonder of it all*)

Davie.

QUEEN (*to the Headsman*)
  Davie.

HEADSMAN
  Make way — make way for her Majesty the
  Queen and Sir Davie Little Boy.
  [*They go out.*
  Immediately the Boy returns and gets the pot
  of lentils and runs after the Queen as
                The Curtains Close.

APPENDIX

THE REPERTORY OF THE PORTMAN-
TEAU THEATER

APPENDIX

CASTS

At the Thirty-ninth Street Theater, and the Princess Theater, New York City, During November and December of 1916.

Persons Before the Plays

MEMORY .... *Florence Wollersen*
THE PROLOGUE .... *Lew Medbury*
THE DEVICE-BEARER ..... *Edmond Crenshaw*

The Trimplet

THE LADY CARATINA .... *Gitruda Tristjanski*
THE LADY BOBOLARA .... *Judith Lowry*
THE BARON MILTON-MAU-
    RICE .... *Willard Webster*
THE MARQUESS OF STRE-
    NATHCO .... *Edgar Stehli*
THE PERSON PASSING BY.. *McKay Morris*
YOU .... *Gregory Kelly*

Nevertheless

A BOY .... *Gregory Kelly*
A GIRL .... *Nancy Winston*
A BURGLAR .... *McKay Morris*

Six Who Pass While the Lentils Boil

THE BOY .... *Gregory Kelly*
THE QUEEN .... *Judith Lowry*
THE MIME .... *Willard Webster*
THE MILKMAID .... *Nancy Winston*
THE BLINDMAN .... *Edgar Stehli*
THE BALLAD-SINGER ..... *Stuart Walker*
THE HEADSMAN .... *McKay Morris*

APPENDIX

THE MEDICINE-SHOW

The Medicine-Show was not played in New York City.

LUT'ER .... *Willard Webster*
GIZ .... *Edgar Stehli*
DR. STEV'N VANDEXTER ... *Lew Medbury*